WOI
HISTORY:
Sites & Resources

Featuring 40 Women's History Sites & Projects Plus
Travel Itineraries, Teaching Plans, & Websites

Edited by Heather A. Huyck, Ph.D.

ncwhs
national collaborative for women's history sites

NATIONAL COLLABORATIVE FOR WOMEN'S HISTORY SITES

This guide includes information, photographs, and artwork submitted by organizational members of the National Collaborative for Women's History Sites, and each site holds the individual copyrights. We have made every effort to include accurate information, but, because circumstances change, readers should call or check websites before visiting a site. The Collaborative wishes to thank its partners, the National Park Service and the Organization of American Historians, for their continued support. In particular, we acknowledge the work of the National Park Service, especially Joan Bacharach, Beth Boland, and Carol Schull, in preparing the Museum Management Online Exhibits, the Teaching with Historic Places, and the Travel Itineraries–thank you! Without Margaret "Peg" Strobel, this guide would not be published. To join the NCWHS, please visit our website.

© 2009   National Collaborative for Women's History Sites
Second Edition.   All Rights Reserved.
ISBN: 978-0-9770095-5-8
Library of Congress Control Number: 2009923023

Published by the
National Collaborative for Women's History Sites
http://ncwhs.oah.org

Edited by Heather A. Huyck, Ph.D.
Designed and produced by Robert P. J. Cooney, Jr.
Cover by Dina Clark Design
Printed by Community Printers, Santa Cruz, CA

Available from:
NCWHS through our website: http://ncwhs.oah.org
National Women's History Project at 707-636-2888 or www.nwhp.org
Eastern National Bookstore at www.eparks.com

CREDITS: *Front cover (clockwise from top left)*: Maggie Howard, Yosemite basketmaker, from the Yosemite Research Library; Eleanor Roosevelt's home and garden; Navajo pot by Maria Martinez, from NPS Museum Management Program; A. E. Ted Aub's statue of Elizabeth Cady Stanton being introduced to Susan B. Anthony, Seneca Falls, NY, NPS photo by David Malone; World War II poster honoring Women Ordnance Workers, from Springfield Armory. *Back cover:* Portrait of Martha Washington, Independence NHP; Pearl Buck's library; Maggie L. Walker. *Title page:* World War II tool grinder, from Springfield Armory.

Contents

Introduction

Welcome to the 2nd edition of *Women's History: Sites and Resources*. This book introduces you to the special places that let us experience the past in ways no other historic documents can. When we read, we must visualize the past. At historic places, instead of *imagining* those people who wrote the letters, made the pots, and shaped the land, we can *encounter* those women. Because historic sites are tangible, usually retaining their physical and environmental settings, we can walk into and around once-busy mills, feel dank basements where enslaved women cooked, see the chairs where women famous and unknown once sat (and the beds they actually slept in) and almost touch those pasts. Everyone can enjoy and find inspiration, amazement (and sometimes, horror) at these historic sites.

The National Collaborative for Women's History Sites, an organization advocating the identification, preservation, interpretation, and research of these special places, is pleased to share this heritage of *all of us*, a heritage still too little known (http://ncwhs.oah.org). *Women's History: Sites & Resources* now features 40 historic places and projects of women's past, sites that recognize the significance of fully including women's history. Ironically, many historic places are homes that tell us more about the women who lived there than the men whose fame encouraged their preservation. Every historic site—from battlefield to armory, library to prison, tenement to factory—includes women's history, directly or indirectly.

We also include places to visit *virtually* on the web, places for teaching and traveling, as well as museum objects and an expanded bibliography. While nothing compares to actually being there—encountering these places firsthand—we have done the preliminary research so that you may more easily find and enjoy them.

Mrs. Betsy Augusta Penniman, 19th-century whaling ship Captain Edward Penniman's wife, sailed their ship 100 miles during a storm to retrieve her husband who had gone ashore. Just as she sailed on, we believe it crucial to find women's history, or as one historian said, "the majority finds its past." We invite you to join us.

Heather A. Huyck, editor

WOMEN'S HISTORY:
Sites & Resources

Sites & resources appear geographically, west to east.

Top left: Portrait of Lucretia Mott.
Center: Old Courthouse, site of the Dred Scott and Virginia Minor cases.
Right: Frederick Douglass's armchair, slippers, cane, and dumbbells.
Bottom row: Frances Willard House; painting in The Stowe Center.

Topical Index to Women's History: Sites & Resources

Listed in alphabetical order by name of organization or last name of individua

Regions

West

Arizona Women's Heritage Trail
Boggsville Historic Site
Grace Hudson Museum
National Women's History Project
Rosie the Riveter/WWII Home Front NHP
Woman Suffrage Media Project
Yosemite National Park

Midwest

Jane Addams Hull-House Museum
Chicago Area Women's History Council
Chicago Women's Liberation Union Herstory Project
Evanston Women's History Project
Ulysses S. Grant NHS
Jefferson National Expansion Memorial
Naper Settlement
Oberlin Heritage Center
Bonniebrook, Rose O'Neill's Home
Women's History Tours of the Twin Cities

South

Maggie Walker NHS
George Washington Birthplace National Monument

Mid-Atlantic

American Swedish Historical Museum
Clara Barton NHS
Mary McLeod Bethune Council House NHS
Pearl S. Buck House NHL
Frederick Douglass NHS
General Federation of Women's Clubs
Independence NHP
Nathaniel Newlin Grist Mill
New Century Trust
Paulsdale NHL
Sewall-Belmont House & Museum

Northeast

Eleanor Roosevelt NHS
Farmington Quaker Meetinghouse
Matilda Joslyn Gage Home
Minute Man NHP
Kate Mullany NHS/ALSC
Nantucket Maria Mitchell Association
Springfield Armory NHS
Harriet Beecher Stowe Center
Martin Van Buren NHS
Women's Rights NHP

Fields

African Americans

Mary McLeod Bethune Council House NHS (National Council of Negro Women, organizing)
Farmington Quaker Meetinghouse (Underground RR)
Frederick Douglass NHS (slavery to freedom)
Matilda Joslyn Gage Home (Underground RR)

Ulysses S. Grant NHS
(enslaved people)
Independence NHP
Jefferson National Expansion
Memorial
Oberlin Heritage Center
Springfield Armory NHS
(employment)
Stowe Center (Anti-Slavery)
Maggie Walker NHS
Women's Rights NHP
(Underground RR)

Archeology

Boggsville Historic Site
Ulysses S. Grant NHS
Independence NHP
George Washington Birthplace
National Monument

Archives

Mary McLeod Bethune Council
House NHS (National Archives
for Black Women's History)
Chicago Women's Liberation
Union Herstory Project
Oberlin Heritage Center
Minute Man NHP
Maggie Walker NHS
Sewall-Belmont House &
Museum

Hispanics/Latinas

Arizona Women's Heritage Trail
Boggsville Historic Site

Immigration

American Swedish Historical
Museum
Jane Addams Hull-House Museum
Martin Van Buren NHS (Irish)

Literary & Artistic Work

Pearl S. Buck House NHL
Grace Hudson Museum
Minute Man NHP/The Wayside
Bonniebrook, Rose O'Neill's Home

Native Americans/Indians

Arizona Women's Heritage Trail
Boggsville Historic Site (Cheyenne)
Farmington Quaker Meetinghouse
(Seneca)
Matilda Joslyn Gage Home
(Iroquois)
Grace Hudson Museum (Pomo)

Organizations

Amer. Labor Studies Center/Kate
Mullany NHS
Chicago Area Women's History
Council
Chicago Women's Liberation Union
Herstory Project
Evanston Women's History Project
General Federation of Women's
Clubs
National Collaborative for Women's
History Sites
National Park Service
National Women's History Project
New Century Trust
Oberlin Heritage Center
Woman Suffrage Media Project

Political History and Wars

Chicago Area Women's History
Council
Chicago Women's Liberation
Union Herstory Project
Frederick Douglass NHS
Matilda Joslyn Gage Home
Ulysses S. Grant NHS
Independence NHP

Minute Man NHP
Eleanor Roosevelt NHS
Rosie the Riveter/WWII Home
    Front NHP
Springfield Armory NHS
Women's Rights NHP

Religious History

Farmington Quaker Meetinghouse
    (Quaker)
Independence NHP (Episcopal,
    Quaker)
Nantucket Maria Mitchell
    Association (Quaker)
Maggie Walker NHS (Baptist)

Scientific & Technological History

Jane Addams Hull-House Museum
    (sociology)
Grace Hudson Museum
    (ethnography)
Nantucket Maria Mitchell
    Association (astronomy)
Nathaniel Newlin Grist Mill
    (technology)
Yosemite National Park (botany)

Social Reform

Jane Addams Hull-House Museum
Mary McLeod Bethune Council
    House NHS
Clara Barton NHS
Frederick Douglass NHS
Evanston Women's History Project
Matilda Joslyn Gage Home
General Federation of Women's
    Clubs
Kate Mullany NHS/ALSC
New Century Trust
Paulsdale NHL
Eleanor Roosevelt NHS
Sewall-Belmont House & Museum
Harriet Beecher Stowe Center

Maggie Walker NHS
Women's Rights NHP

Suffragists/Women's Rights

Jane Addams Hull-House Museum
Frederick Douglass NHS
Matilda Joslyn Gage Home
Jefferson National Expansion
    Memorial
Bonniebrook, Rose O'Neill's Home
Oberlin Heritage Center
Paulsdale NHL
Sewall-Belmont House & Museum
Woman Suffrage Media Project
Women's Rights NHP

Trails & Tours

Arizona Women's Heritage Trail
Evanston Women's History Project
Women's History Tours of the Twin
    Cities
See also Resources Section, page 91

Time Periods/Emphasis

17th Century

American Swedish Historical
    Museum
George Washington Birthplace
    National Monument

18th Century

American Swedish Historical
    Museum
Independence NHP
Minute Man NHP
Nathaniel Newlin Grist Mill
George Washington Birthplace
    National Monument

19th Century

American Swedish Historical Museum

Clara Barton NHS (and American Red Cross)

Boggsville Historic Site

Evanston Women's History Project

Frederick Douglass NHS (Anna Murray Douglass, Helen Pitt Douglass)

Farmington Quaker Meetinghouse

Matilda Joslyn Gage Home

Ulysses S. Grant NHS (& Julia Dent Grant)

General Federation of Women's Clubs

Grace Hudson Museum

Jefferson National Expansion Memorial

Minute Man NHP

Kate Mullany NHS/ALSC (National Labor Union)

Naper Settlement

Nantucket Maria Mitchell Assoc.

Nathaniel Newlin Grist Mill

New Century Trust

Oberlin Heritage Center (Lucy Stone)

Sewall-Belmont House & Museum

Harriet Beecher Stowe Center

Martin Van Buren NHS

Maggie Walker NHS

Woman Suffrage Media Project

Women's Rights NHP (Elizabeth Cady Stanton, Frederick Douglass, Lucretia Mott)

Yosemite National Park

20th Century

American Swedish Historical Museum

Jane Addams Hull-House Museum

Arizona Women's Heritage Trail

Mary McLeod Bethune Council House NHS (National Council of Negro Women)

Pearl S. Buck House NHL

Chicago Area Women's History Council

Chicago Women's Liberation Union Herstory Project

Evanston Women's History Project

General Federation of Women's Clubs

Minute Man NHP

Naper Settlement

National Women's History Project

Nathaniel Newlin Grist Mill

New Century Trust

Bonniebrook, Rose O'Neill's Home

Paulsdale NHL

Eleanor Roosevelt NHS

Rosie the Riveter/WWII Home Front NHP

Sewall-Belmont House & Museum (National Woman's Party)

Springfield Armory NHS

Maggie Walker NHS (Independent Order of St. Luke)

Woman Suffrage Media Project

Women's History Tours of the Twin Cities

Yosemite National Park

Grace Hudson Museum & Sun House

UKIAH, CALIFORNIA

Grace Carpenter Hudson and her dog Mascot, c. 1895.

Regional art and culture in the tradition of an extraordinary family

The Grace Hudson Museum, an art, history, and anthropology museum, focuses on the lifeworks of nationally admired artist Grace Carpenter Hudson (1865-1937) and her husband, self-trained anthropologist Dr. John Hudson (1857-1936). Their shared life goal was the documentation of local Pomo Indian peoples' culture and history. Other members of the Carpenter-Hudson family contributed importantly to regional history and various American reform movements, including advocating for women's rights and abolition.

FACILITIES

The Grace Hudson Museum, with its four modern exhibition galleries, provides opportunities for art appreciation, historical reflection, and cultural enrichment. An enclosed courtyard showcases native plants used by Pomo Indian peoples for food, medicine, and the creation of basketry and other

DON'T MISS

- Pomo Indian Basketry Gallery
- Unique gift shop
- Grace's Bell Tower

tools of daily life. Adjacent to the museum is the Sun House, the Hudsons' furnished 1911 redwood Craftsman bungalow, and its grounds, which are open for guided tours.

PROGRAMS

The Museum displays and interprets objects from the multi-faceted estate of this exceptional family in both long-term and short-term exhibitions, using them as a springboard for contemporary examinations of a variety of cultural and artistic themes. Diverse scheduled public educational programs and tours further illuminate these exhibition themes.

COLLECTIONS

The Museum holds the largest collection of Grace Hudson's artwork; John Hudson's ethnographic field notebooks and unpublished manuscripts on California Indian tribes, particularly Pomo Indian peoples; significant holdings of Pomo Indian artifacts, especially basketry; thousands of glass plate negatives and historic prints from the photography business of Grace Hudson's parents, A. O. and Helen Carpenter, depicting the people and places of 19th-century rural northern California's Mendocino County; and the

"My canvases are unique."

– Grace Carpenter Hudson

Grace Hudson's paintings on display in the Museum's gallery dedicated to her artwork.

writings of Grace's mother, Helen McCowen Carpenter, on the early European American settlement of Mendocino County.

Grace Hudson Museum
& Sun House
431 South Main Street
Ukiah, CA 59482
707-467-2836
gracehudson@pacific.net
www.gracehudsonmuseum.org

Open year round.
Check hours before visiting.
Wednesday – Saturday 10 a.m. – 4:30 p.m.
Sunday noon – 4:30 p.m.
Admission fee:
$4 per person, $10 per family

13

Rosie the Riveter/ WWII Home Front National Historical Park

RICHMOND, CALIFORNIA

Dedicated to the countless Americans—including women—in Richmond, California, and across the nation, whose work and sacrifices on the "home front" helped achieve World War II victory

Americans won victory in World War II with huge and coordinated efforts on both battlefields and "home front." Americans of all ages and backgrounds worked

---

DON'T MISS

- SS *Red Oak Victory*, last of the World War II ships built at Shipyard No. 3
- Historical markers and spectacular views along the Bay Trail

Home Front Youth Corps in front of the SS *Red Oak Victory* at Shipyard No. 3.

in factories, shipyards, and victory gardens. Long expected to stay at home, women were now asked to do heavy industrial jobs building ships, planes, and tanks. Eighteen million women known as "Rosies" (after a popular World War II song, "Rosie the Riveter") entered the defense industry in unprecedented numbers, working as riveters, welders, and in other nontraditional jobs. The park preserves the stories, industrial production facilities, and social institutions (day care and health care) that were all part of the total war effort. Home front workers often shared inadequate housing and worked physically difficult

14

and dangerous jobs to "bring the boys home."

FACILITIES

A "partnership park," Rosie the Riveter/WWII Home Front NHP collaborates closely with the city of Richmond, California, to preserve and interpret sites citywide. Key sites located along Richmond's coastline include: historic Shipyard No. 3, the Ford Assembly Building (the park

Park banner.

visitor center opens there in 2010), and the Rosie the Riveter Memorial in its Marina Bay Park.

PROGRAMS

Regular interpretive tours are offered year round at the Rosie the Riveter Memorial and via bus to park sites. For ship tours, see www.ssredoakvictory.com.

COLLECTIONS

The over 11,000-item collection includes 4,500 oral histories, photographs, scrapbooks, publications, vintage posters, ship-launch programs, letters, food ration books, war bond stamps, USO and Civil Service materials, and a variety of work-related items, such as shipyard badges, uniforms, and tools. The site is accessible for students, researchers, and the public; some items will be exhibited at the park's visitor center.

Rosie the Riveter/
WWII Home Front
National Historical Park
1401 Marina Way South
Richmond, CA 94804
(temporary visitor center)
510-232-5050

For current visitor information, see
www.nps.gov/rori.

15

National Women's History Project

SANTA ROSA, CALIFORNIA

Participants discuss women's history at a NWHP Networking Conference.

National Women's History Project

Your portal for women's history information, resources, and materials

The **National Women's History Project** was founded in 1980 in northern California after local women began

---

DON'T MISS

- Award-winning website, web store, and speakers bureau
- Links to women's history performers and historic sites
- Women's History Month activities every March

exploring and celebrating women's history in the neighborhood schools. In 1987 the NWHP led a coalition that successfully lobbied Congress to designate March as National Women's History Month, which is now officially celebrated nationwide. The NWHP was also an original founder of the National Collaborative for Women's History Sites.

FACILITIES

While not literally an historic site, the NWHP is a significant center for work today that helps move women forward. The Project champions the accomplishments of multicultural American women through publications, presentations, conferences, panels, a popular website (www.nwhp.org), and an annual catalog of Women's History Resources. The NWHP's networks also help extend the range of women's history into many different areas of society.

PROGRAMS

The National Women's History Project is the catalyst for activities that celebrate multicultural women as leaders and influential forces in our society. Every year the NWHP chooses the overall theme for National Women's History Month, for example "Women: Taking the Lead to Save the Planet," and selects a number of notable American women from diverse backgrounds to honor. Throughout the year, the NWHP develops resources and plans programs that promote a more balanced and inclusive view of history.

COLLECTIONS

The NWHP carries hundreds of resources, including books, posters, DVDs, display sets, and much more, many produced by the Project. The NWHP is also the repository for the Women's History Research Center Microfilm Collections, which contain primary source material produced by the women's movement during the 1960s and 1970s (distributed by Scholarly Resources).

"I long to speak out the intense inspiration that comes to me from the lives of strong women."

– Ruth Benedict

Molly Murphy MacGregor (left) and marchers after the California Equality Day Parade, Sacramento, August 2008.

National Women's History Project
3440 Airway Drive, Suite F
Santa Rosa, CA 95403
707-636-2888
Fax 707-636-2909
nwhp@aol.com
www.nwhp.org

9 a.m. - 5 a.m. Monday - Friday
Molly Murphy MacGregor,
Executive Director and Co-founder

Woman Suffrage Media Project

SANTA CRUZ, CALIFORNIA

Championing the heritage of the American woman suffrage movement

The spectacular campaigns that won basic civil rights for American women stand out as highpoints in our nation's history. The inspirational power and influence of the woman suffrage movement live on, encouraging the nonviolent democratic efforts of women and men today.

DON'T MISS

- *Winning the Vote*, by Robert P. J. Cooney, Jr.
- Website includes photographs, resources, reviews, and more
- Online article on "Taking a New Look at the Woman Suffrage Movement"

Susan B. Anthony, president of the National American Woman Suffrage Association between 1892 and 1900, on the porch of her Rochester, NY, home.

HISTORY

The **Woman Suffrage Media Project** (WSMP) was created in 1993 to generate interest in this exceptional chapter in American history, which lasted from 1848 to 1920. Working closely with the National Women's History Project, the WSMP encouraged celebrations of the 75th and 85th anniversaries, in 1995 and 2005, of the 19th [Woman Suffrage] Amendment to the U.S. Constitution. These national events helped re-establish this movement as an important part of our past that deserves greater recognition today.

As one of the few centers specializing in the woman

suffrage movement, the WSMP offers research and consulting services, speakers, publications, and presentations on suffrage history and personalities. The Project has assisted with several books, publications, and videos, including the PBS film *One Woman, One Vote*; the Ken Burns documentary *Not for Ourselves Alone*; and the Huntington Library video *Votes for Women*.

In 2005, Project director Robert P. J. Cooney, Jr. published *Winning the Vote: The Triumph of the American Woman Suffrage Movement* with American

involvement.

The WSMP plans special presentations annually highlighting events in suffrage history, such as the 90th anniversary of the 19th Amendment in 2010 and the centennial of women winning the vote in California in 2011. A beautiful poster reprinted from the successful 1911 campaign is now available (from www.nwhp.org), with further projects and publications forthcoming.

COLLECTIONS

The WSMP houses an extensive library of books, magazines, reference material, ephemera, artifacts, subject and article files, and over a thousand illustrations and photographic prints from sources across the country. Researchers by appointment.

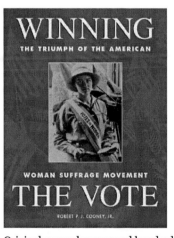

Original research uncovered hundreds of suffrage photographs, campaign posters, cartoons and other images.

Graphic Press. This popular history, over twelve years in the making, reproduces hundreds of rare photographs, posters, and illustrations documenting women's early political

Woman Suffrage Media Project
Robert P. J. Cooney, Jr., Director
PO Box 8403
Santa Cruz, CA 95061
831-423-8436
RobertCooney@ebold.com
www.AmericanGraphicPress.com

Yosemite National Park

YOSEMITE, CALIFORNIA

Discover Yosemite's women—basketweavers, explorers, naturalists, homesteaders, business women, and park rangers

Clare Marie Hodges, first woman park ranger, hired in 1918. Photo courtesy of Yosemite Research Library.

Yosemite National Park covers nearly 1,200 square miles of mountainous terrain in the Sierra Nevada of California. A wilderness park best known for its waterfalls, deep valleys, grand meadows, and ancient giant sequoias, Yosemite also has a rich cultural history in which women have played important—though often hidden—parts. Native women lived there for thousands of years; their basketry is now exhibited. Jessie Benton Frémont's adventures and written descriptions of Yosemite Valley and the Mariposa Grove of Big Trees influenced its early preservation efforts. Laundresses accompanied the U.S. Army stationed there. Clothing reforms such as the advent of "bloomers" helped women to participate in outdoor pursuits. Women's domestic skills sometimes became profitable businesses;

DON'T MISS

- Park introductory film, *Spirit of Yosemite* (Yosemite Valley Visitor Center)
- Yosemite Museum/Indian Village of Ahwahnee
- Pioneer Yosemite History Center in Wawona

20

female homesteaders helped support their families by selling baked bread. Widowed, Jennie "Mother" Foster Curry continued to run Camp Curry. Claire Marie Hodges served as the first female National Park Service Park Ranger, and female ranger-naturalists searched Yosemite's heights, discovering previously unknown species such as the Yosemite bog orchid.

FACILITIES

With 263 miles of roads, over 700 miles of hiking trails, and hundreds of species of birds mammals, flowering plants, and trees, Yosemite has much to see and do. While open, some areas are seasonally inaccessible due to snow. Reservations are not required to enter Yosemite, but lodging reservations are strongly recommended.

Maggie Howard and her baskets. Photo courtesy of Yosemite Research Library.

"In due time I awoke to the glory and grandeur of that wonderful valley, of which no descriptions nor paintings can give the least idea."

– Elizabeth Cady Stanton,
Eighty Years and More

PROGRAMS

Information about American Indian women and pioneers in Yosemite can be viewed at several interpretive exhibits. Visit www.nps.gov/yose/historyculture to learn more: see the podcast "Wildflower" about Enid Michael and current NPS botanists. Download "Notable Women in Yosemite's History." Attend free ranger programs, including some specific to Yosemite's women's history.

Yosemite National Park
PO Box 577
9039 Village Drive
Yosemite, California 95389
209-372-0200
www.nps.gov/yose

Arizona Women's Heritage Trail

ARIZONA

Sharlot Hall, Arizona's Territorial Historian. Courtesy of Sharlot Hall Museum, Prescott, Arizona.

A statewide project expanding and linking women's history and historic sites

Women have made major contributions to the development of Arizona, but their stories are missing from its history. Arizona only became a state in 1912. Its territorial history was full of ranching, mining for gold and copper, and Native American tribes (including Hopi, Navajo, Pima, Papago, and Apache).

DON'T MISS

- The Arizona Women's Heritage Trail web exhibit at www.womens heritagetrail.org

Arizona rancher Sandra Day O'Conner became the first woman on the U.S. Supreme Court; decades before, in 1950, Arizona Democrats nominated Ana Froh Miller for governor but she lost.

The Arizona Women's Heritage Trail will link women's history to historic sites throughout the state, featuring, for example, Rebecca Dallis, who taught African American students in a one-room schoolhouse, segregated until 1952, while earning one-third the pay European American teachers received. Meet Viola Jimulla, renowned basket weaver and, in 1940, Chieftess (sic) of the Yavapai Prescott Indian tribe. And Isabella Greenway, Arizona's first congresswoman, who served from 1933-36. The Trail will use maps, a website, and other resources to educate the general public about women's leadership, promote women's history, and increase Arizona's tourism.

HISTORY

Launched in fall 2005 through a coalition of Arizona historical agencies and women's organizations, the Arizona Women's Heritage Trail (AWHT) formed a collaboration with Arizona State University's Institute for Humanities Research of the College of Liberal Arts and Sciences. Recently designated a legacy program by the Arizona State Centennial Commission, the Trail actively involves the community, universities, and schools through its outreach, while showcasing the state's multicultural heritage.

Governor's Mansion restored by Ms. Sharlot Hall and campus of the Sharlot Hall Museum in Prescott, Arizona. Eventually a museum was created around it. Courtesy of Sharlot Hall Museum.

PROGRAMS

AWHT is currently developing a statewide traveling exhibit, regional driving and local walking tours, tourist maps, a fourth-grade school curriculum, historic site interpretive signage, and publications about contributions of the rich diversity of Arizona women. Project leaders and historians meet with cultural representatives of Arizona's 22 American Indian tribes to include native women. The Trail will also represent the heritages of African American, Hispanic American, Asian American, and European American women.

STRUCTURE

The AWHT boards—a Coordinating Council, Scholars and Researchers Board, and an Advisory Board—include academics, public historians, archivists, preservationists, tribal government officials, and leaders from throughout the state. The governor serves as honorary chair.

Arizona Women's Heritage Trail
18743 East Bravo Lane
Rio Verde, AZ 85263
480-471-7792
womensheritagetr@aol.com
www.womensheritagetrail.org

Boggsville Historic Site

LAS ANIMAS, COLORADO

On the Santa Fe Trail and last home of Kit Carson

Josefa Jaramillo Carson and Kit Carson, Jr., c. 1860. Four Carson children went to Boggsville school. Courtesy Kit Carson Historic Museum.

At **Boggsville Historic Site,** visitors learn about the critical roles women played in life along the Santa Fe Trail, a 900-mile international trade and travel corridor from Missouri to Santa Fe (now in New Mexico) for much of the 19th century. Built on a Mexican land grant, the site was home to Hispanic, Anglo American, and Native American settlers. Today, the 1860s adobe houses of the families of Tom and Rumalda Luna Boggs and of John and Amache Ochinee Prowers show this cultural synergy.

FACILITIES

Currently the site contains a visitor center at the Boggs House and a self-guided trail. A modern restroom with showers, three RV parking spaces, and camping are available, along with a kitchen for events and field schools. The houses are open from May through October.

DON'T MISS

- Boggsville "Trade Room" and self-guided trails

PROGRAMS

Both houses contain exhibits. The Boggs House "Trade Room" displays trade items, original furniture used at Boggsville, and an interpretive room. The Prowers House has a display on the Santa Fe Trail (in progress) and a meeting room. The site is often used to train students in archeological research, with excavations open to the public. Summertime evening programs are offered.

COLLECTIONS

A rich architectural legacy, the restored adobe houses blend Hispanic, Anglo, and Cheyenne architectural traditions. Ongoing

Boggs House and interpretive display panel.

historical archeology gives Boggsville a growing collection of artifacts. Additionally, the Boggsville Library houses archeological reports from years of excavation and other documents.

Prowers House at Boggsville, built in 1867, faces east toward the sunrise, Cheyenne style. John Prower's wife, Amache Ochinee Prowers, was a daughter of a Cheyenne leader.

Boggsville Historic Site
PO Box 68
Las Animas, CO 81054
719-456-1358
boggsville67@yahoo.com

Located two miles south of Las Animas on Colorado Highway 101. During May, open Wednesday – Sunday, 10 a.m. – 4 p.m. Memorial Day through Labor Day open daily, 10 a.m. – 4 p.m. September and October open Wednesday – Sunday, 10 a.m. – 4 p.m.
Check hours before visiting.

Bonniebrook, Home of Rose Cecil O'Neill

WALNUT SHADE, MISSOURI

The historic homestead property of an extraordinary artist, author, activist, suffragist, and philanthropist

Rose Cecil O'Neill.

Rose Cecil O'Neill (1874-1944) produced thousands of illustrations and was among the highest paid female illustrators during her career. Her sculpture and paintings were exhibited in Paris and New York. O'Neill wrote four novels, numerous short stories, eight children's books, and one book of poetry. An ardent suffragist, O'Neill actively participated in the women's suffrage movement. In 1909, she created the famous Kewpie character in her Bonniebrook art studio. Kewpie cartoons became O'Neill's voice for political activism and human rights. By 1913, sales of Kewpie dolls and figurines made O'Neill an instant millionaire.

FACILITIES

Visitor's center has the museum and art gallery, research library, gift shop, meeting rooms, and administrative offices. The rebuilt home includes antique furniture, original art, photographs, and personal items belonging to O'Neill. Beautiful gardens, walking trails, and wooden foot bridges are located throughout the property. Rose O'Neill, her

---

DON'T MISS

- O'Neill's original art
- Exceptional museum and art gallery
- O'Neill family cemetery
- Garden exhibit of O'Neill limestone sculptures

mother, two sisters, and two brothers are buried in the O'Neill family cemetery.

PROGRAMS

Guided tours of the home and museum interpret the history of Rose O'Neill. Educational tours for students, teachers, and researchers are available on request. The site encourages artists to bring their easels and enjoy the beautiful walking trails and solitude that provide the perfect backdrop for creative minds. An annual open house—free to the public—lets everyone discover Bonniebrook's enchantment.

"Bonniebrook is my favorite place on earth."

– Rose Cecil O'Neill

Suffrage Kewpie post card.

Bonniebrook Tour Home.

COLLECTIONS

The museum contains original art, letters, poems, books, thousands of Kewpie dolls, and other historic O'Neill memorabilia. Open to the public by appointment, the research library has an estimated 20,000 pages of archived letters, clippings, manuscripts, photographs, and other documents of her history. Two O'Neill oversized limestone sculptures are displayed where she placed them on the front lawn of Bonniebrook.

Bonniebrook Historical Society
485 Rose O'Neill Road
Walnut Shade, MO 65616
800-539-7437
www.roseoneill.org

Open 9 -4 p.m. Tuesday - Saturday
Open April 1 - December 1.
Check hours before visiting.

Ulysses S. Grant National Historic Site

ST. LOUIS, MISSOURI

The St. Louis home of Civil War General and 18th President Ulysses S. Grant and his wife Julia Dent Grant

Julia Dent Grant, a partner, friend, and confidante to her husband throughout their lives together.

Ulysses S. Grant National Historic Site, historically known as White Haven, was the childhood home of Julia Dent, who married Grant in 1848. While the site is named after the famous Union general and 18th president, park interpretation and education includes his wife of 37 years, as well as the enslaved men and women who labored on the farm during Julia Dent Grant's father's ownership.

DON'T MISS

- The main house to learn about the perspectives and lives of White Haven's residents
- The museum, where the Grants' lives are placed within their tumultuous historical times

FACILITIES

The site has five historic structures: the main house; a stone summer kitchen and laundry building; a chicken house; an ice house; and a stable, now the site's museum. A new visitor center contains exhibits, an introductory film, restrooms, a classroom, and a sales area.

PROGRAMS

Visitors may take ranger-led tours of the main house and outbuildings, view the introductory film, and explore "An Intricate Tapestry: The Lives of Ulysses and Julia Grant" in the interpretive museum. On- and off-site education programs and traveling trunks can be reserved for K-12 students, Elderhostel students, and community groups. A Junior Ranger program is available for children ages 5-15, and special programs and exhibits are offered throughout the year.

White Haven, Julia Dent Grant's childhood home. She married Ulysses S. Grant in 1848. Three of their four children were born on the White Haven estate.

COLLECTIONS

The site's main collections consist of architectural elements preserved from the historic structures during the restoration and numerous artifacts retrieved during extensive archeological investigations. The library has over 1400 monographs and 1200 items in vertical files. Because enslaved people made and used many of these artifacts, the site's collection is excellent for interpreting Midwestern slave life.

In the dank winter kitchen, visitors learn about the enslaved women and children who lived and worked at White Haven.

Ulysses S. Grant
National Historic Site
7400 Grant Road
St. Louis, MO 63123
314-842-3298
www.nps.gov/ulsg

Check hours before visiting.
Open 9 a.m. – 5 p.m. daily.
Closed Thanksgiving, Christmas, and New Year's.

Jefferson National Expansion Memorial

ST. LOUIS, MISSOURI

Virginia Minor.

Restored courtrooms recall famous trials

Built between 1839 and 1862, **St. Louis' Old Courthouse** was the site of two Dred Scott trials in 1847 and 1850 and the Virginia Minor case in 1872. While Dred Scott is well known, few people realize that his wife Harriet separately sued for her freedom. Because slave status followed the mother, their daughters' freedom was also denied. The U.S. Supreme Court *Dred Scott* decision of 1857 proved inflam-matory, moving this nation towards the Civil War as it denied black slaves their rights as U.S. citizens. Dred Scott died in 1858; Harriet Scott, who lived to 1876, later gained her freedom.

In 1872, Virginia Minor, an officer in the National Woman Suffrage Association, tried to register to vote but was refused. Minor sued. She lost her case in the Missouri lower and Supreme Courts and appealed it to the U.S. Supreme Court. In October 1874, the Supreme Court unanimously ruled in *Minor v. Happersett* that "the Constitution of the United States does not confer the right of suffrage upon anyone."

DON'T MISS

- *Slavery on Trial* film about the Scotts and Lucy Delany, who also sued for freedom
- Exhibit "Dred Scott: A Legacy of Courage"
- Museum store featuring these trials, civil rights, and African American history

FACILITIES

The Old Courthouse includes the original sites of the trials of Dred and Harriet Scott and Virginia

Minor, including two restored courtrooms. Four exhibit galleries outline St. Louis history; a separate gallery examines the Scott and Minor cases.

PROGRAMS

Programs at the Old Courthouse include ranger-guided, scripted trial reenactments presented within an original courtroom, where the public or educational groups can participate. For group programs, call for advance reservations.

COLLECTIONS

The original courtroom where Virginia Minor's case was tried is now the park's library and archives; it houses books and resources with copies of court documents relating to the Courthouse and its historic cases, including women tried for assisting slave escapes.

"It is impossible that this can be a republican government, in which one-half the citizens thereof are forever disenfranchised."

– Virginia Minor

Old Courthouse and Arch.

Jefferson National Expansion Memorial
11 North Fourth Street
St. Louis, MO 63102
314-655-1700
www.nps.gov/jeff

Check hours before visiting. The Old Courthouse is open daily from 8:00 a.m. to 4:30 p.m., except Thanksgiving, Christmas, and New Year's Day.

Harriet and Dred Scott.

31

Naper Settlement/ Naperville Heritage Society

NAPERVILLE, ILLINOIS

Caroline Martin Mitchell.

Naper Settlement, an outdoor history museum, includes the Martin Mitchell Mansion and its carriage house

Caroline Martin Mitchell, the youngest daughter of an influential **Naperville** early 19th-century pioneer family, bequeathed her Victorian home and surrounding 212 acres to the City of Naperville in 1936. Her home is now part of Naper Settlement, an outdoor history museum, accredited by the American Association of Museums and administered by the Naperville Heritage Society, located in suburban Naperville. The museum shows how Naperville and Midwestern towns like it grew from frontier outposts to bustling centers of commerce and industry.

FACILITIES

Visitors to Naper Settlement can see 30 historic structures in a beautifully landscaped 12-acre village setting. During the summer season, April through October, costumed villagers interpret and recreate domestic, craft, and commercial life, ranging from the 1830s to the early 1900s. The 1883 Martin

---

DON'T MISS

- Completely restored Martin Mitchell Mansion
- Ongoing exhibit "Brushstrokes of the Past: Naperville's Story"
- Costumed villagers from April-October
- Hands-on history for children ages 3-10

Mitchell Mansion and carriage house are listed on the National Register of Historic Places and open for visitors during the summer season and for special events.

PROGRAMS

Community outreach emphasizing historic preservation has been a cornerstone of Naper Settlement since its 1969 founding. Programs include the History Speaks Lecture Series, featuring prominent historical people, events, and topics. Annual special events that draw thousands of people include Civil War Days, Naper Days, All Hallows Eve, and Sweet Holidays. Architectural walking tours of historic Naperville neighborhoods also are held during the year, and three self-guided tours are available free-of-charge at the museum and on the website.

COLLECTIONS

The extensive Naper Settlement research library and archives are available to the public by appointment. Letters, diaries, photographic images, newspapers, scrapbooks, deeds, abstracts, manuscripts, books, and periodicals cover Naperville's history from the 19th century to the present day. The Naperville Heritage Society's permanent collections include more than 34,000 two- and three-dimensional items. Many museum artifacts are displayed in settings at Naper Settlement that show their original use.

Naper Settlement
523 South Webster Street
Naperville, IL 60540
630-420-6010
Fax 630-305-4044
towncrier@naperville.il.us
www.napersettlement.museum

Check hours before visiting.
Open April through October, 10 a.m. - 4 p.m. Tuesday-Saturday, 1 - 4 p.m. Sunday. November through March, 10 a.m. - 4 p.m. Monday - Friday. Closed Thanksgiving, Christmas, and New Year's.

Martin Mitchell Mansion.

33

Evanston Women's History Project

EVANSTON, ILLINOIS

EVANSTON WOMEN'S HISTORY PROJECT

Highlighting women's contributions to Evanston's history

Frances Willard, 1873, as the first Dean of Women at Northwestern University. Willard led the Woman's Christian Temperance Union, later headquartered in Evanston.

The **Evanston Women's History Project** unites organizations throughout the Evanston community that have interests in women and U.S./women's history. Evanston, Illinois, just north of Chicago and a university town, has long been known for civic activism.

Project Partners include the Evanston Community Foundation, the Evanston History Center, the Evanston Public Library, the Frances Willard Historical Association, Shorefront, the Woman's Club of Evanston, and the YWCA Evanston/North Shore.

WHAT WILL THE PROJECT DO?

The Project will focus on three areas of work: increasing knowledge, building leadership, and growing Evanston as a tourist destination.

The Project will work to increase knowledge of women's contributions to Evanston history through community programming and increased access to research collections by producing:

o A comprehensive database of Evanston women

DON'T MISS

- The chance to participate in shaping how local women and their achievements are seen historically
- Tour the lovely, historic Frances Willard House

34

- A thematic historic district
- Research resources for women's history scholars
- Women's history month curriculum for schools

The Project will build leadership through participation in programs empowering women and girls today, using the history to inspire future leaders. Outcomes will include:

- Girls' leadership materials
- Leadership programs for women

Finally, the Project will develop Evanston as a tourist destination by providing public access to this history through dynamic and interactive tourism materials and programs, including:

- Maps, brochures, walking tours, and site markers
- A comprehensive website
- A center for women's history located at the Frances Willard House

"The world is wide, and I will not waste my life in friction when it could be turned into momentum."

— **Frances E. Willard**

Visiting Nurses Association.

Evanston Women's
History Project
1730 Chicago Avenue
Evanston, IL 60201
847-328-7500
ewhp@sbcglobal.net
www.evanstonwomen.word
press.com
franceswillardhouse.org

Check hours before visiting.
Tours of the Frances Willard House
First and Third Saturdays of every
month and by special appointment.

Frances Willard House, Evanston, IL.

Chicago Area Women's History Council

CHICAGO, ILLINOIS

A network of historians, archivists, teachers, museum professionals, scholars, preservationists, activists, and others interested in the research, interpretation, and preservation of Chicago women's history

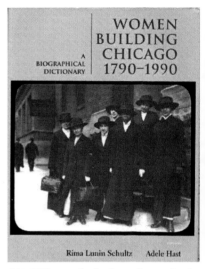

CAWHC's award-winning reference book.

HISTORY

Founded in 1971, the **Chicago Area Women's History Council** is a pioneer volunteer, non-profit organization supporting research, writing, teaching, preservation, and dissemination of women's history. Through the years, CAWHC has sponsored con-ferences, workshops, seminars, lectures, and other educational programs. It developed the first women's history bus tour in Chicago and published the first walking tours of the city's neigh-borhoods highlighting the con-tributions of women. In the late 1980s, CAWHC initiated a major research and writing project that became *Women Building Chicago 1790–1990, A Biographical Dictionary,* published by Indiana University Press in 2001. This award- winning book, edited by Rima Lunin Schultz and Adele Hast, contains 423 biographies and is the best scholarly resource available on Chicago women.

DOCUMENTING THE WOMEN'S MOVEMENT IN CHICAGO, 1960s-1980s

In March 2008, the Chicago Area Women's History Council launched a major new project, Documenting the Women's Movement in Chicago, 1960s–1980s. During this period, Chicago was a vital center of organizational activity that influenced the women's movement both regionally and nationally.

CAWHC will serve as a central registry for information about resources and as a catalyst for community projects. An online searchable database, accessible to all, will identify information and archival resources to study the women's movement. CAWHC is currently surveying existing archival resources and locating privately held materials. The project will also support collecting oral history interviews with significant persons active in, or influenced by, the movement.

SCOPE OF PROJECT

The project embraces feminism in all of its diversity, including advocates of equal rights, equal opportunity, women's liberation, social feminism, lesbian, radical, socialist, and liberal feminism. It takes a multicultural, multiethnic, and multiracial approach. Work of feminist artists, theologians, and other cultural leaders who created a revolution in many areas of American life will also be considered.

Erin McCarthy, oral historian, Sara Evans, historian, Mary Jean Collins, activist, and Beth Myers, archivist, discuss Chicago's role in the Second Wave of the Women's Movement.

Chicago Area
Women's History Council
2109 North Humboldt Boulevard
Chicago, IL 60647
773-227-0093
majohnson@cawhc.org
www.cawhc.org

Mary Ann Johnson, President

Audience members listen to speakers at the Project launch, Chicago History Museum, March 2008.

Chicago Women's Liberation Union Herstory Project

CHICAGO, ILLINOIS

A sample of the historical material now available online at www.cwluherstory.org.

An online historical archive of women's liberation in Chicago

"Sisterhood is powerful" was a vision charged with emotion and energy in the early days of the women's liberation movement. As the **Chicago Women's Liberation Union** (CWLU) blossomed, its hundreds of volunteers provided support, advocacy, information, and service for women and tried new ways of restructuring the world.

DON'T MISS

- Historical documents, photos, posters, music, and more now online at www.cwluherstory.org
- Downloadable show on the women's health movement in Chicago

HISTORY

The Chicago Women's Liberation Union was the umbrella organization of the women's liberation movement in Chicago from 1969 until 1977. The CWLU organized in Chicago's working-class neighborhoods and other communities to build a movement for gender equality and to overcome divisions of race and sexual orientation. At one point, the CWLU had over 30 work groups and chapters. In 1999, former members decided to create a website to share this legacy with next generations so that they can build upon the CWLU's experience to continue the struggle for justice and equality.

COLLECTIONS

The exciting CWLU website hosts a rich collection–hundreds of pages of historic feminist writings, documents (not only from the CWLU), memoirs, interviews, photos, newspapers, letters, art, posters, music, and video. Students use the site for school projects, and professors routinely assign readings from it.

The Herstory Project offers reprints of women's liberation posters from the '70s.

The Project will make this information more available and accessible. Visitors to the website learn about the CWLU's structure, goals, projects, multiple strategies and tactics, successes, and failures. Former CWLU members, activists, and friends tell their stories through audio, video, photos, and written text. Younger activists can communicate with former members, encouraging inter-generational dialogue. Essays and comments on feminist issues can be posted on the Feminist Salon.

The Center for Research on Women and Gender at the University of Illinois at Chicago sponsors the project, although it has not received university or foundation funding. Interns and student volunteers are essential to the ongoing work. The CWLU Herstory Project needs support to help preserve the living history of feminism.

Chicago Women's Liberation Union Herstory Project
PO Box 661
Oak Park, IL 60303
708-386-7197
infogal@cwluherstory.org
www.cwluherstory.org

Estelle Carol, Coordinator

Jane Addams Hull-House Museum

CHICAGO, ILLINOIS

Jane Addams (1860-1935), c. 1890.

The historic site of Hull-House, where Jane Addams and other social reformers lived and worked

The **Jane Addams Hull-House Museum,** part of the College of Architecture and the Arts at the University of Illinois at Chicago (UIC), serves as a dynamic memorial to social reformer and Nobel Peace Prize recipient Jane Addams and other resident social reformers. Their work influenced the lives of their immigrant neighbors as well as national and international public policy. The museum and its programs connect the work of Hull-House residents to important contemporary social issues.

FACILITIES

Visitors to the Jane Addams Hull-House Museum enter galleries in the original Hull Home (1856), where Jane Addams and Ellen Gates Starr began the world famous Hull-House settlement. Visitors to the site may also see exhibits and watch an orientation film in the Resident's Dining Hall building (1907), the only other remaining structure from the original 13-building complex. A small museum shop and administrative offices are located in the original home.

DON'T MISS

- New orientation video *Hull-House: An Experiment In Democracy*
- "Hull-House History On Call" cell phone exhibit
- Original Hull-House Kilns pottery

PROGRAMS

The Hull-House space has always been a site where the public has gathered to discuss, debate, and build solidarity around the most important critical issues of our times. The Museum continues that tradition and hosts programs with community organizations that are free and open to the public. Programs include: Arts and Democracy Series, Conversations on Peace and Justice, and Hull-House Kitchen.

COLLECTIONS

The Museum maintains a collection of objects associated with Jane Addams, Hull-House, and the surrounding historic neighborhood. Items in the Museum's collection include furnishings, pottery, artwork, textiles, and memorabilia that illuminate these histories. In addition, the Special Collections Department of UIC's Richard J.

"The good we secure for ourselves is precarious and uncertain, is floating in mid-air, until it is secured for all of us and incorporated into our common life."

– Jane Addams

Daley Library holds more than 130 archival collections in its Jane Addams Memorial Collection; these resources are shared with the Museum for research and interpretation.

Jane Addams
Hull-House Museum
800 South Halsted Street
Chicago, IL 60607
312-413-5353
Fax 312-413-2092
jahh@uic.edu
www.hullhousemuseum.org

Check hours before visiting.
Open 10 a.m. - 4 p. m. Tuesday – Friday,
12 p.m. - 4 p.m. Sundays.
Closed Mondays and Saturdays.
Visit our website for holiday closures.

UIC COLLEGE OF
UNIVERSITY OF ILLINOIS AT CHICAGO ARCHITECTURE & THE ARTS

The Jane Addams Hull-House Museum.

Oberlin Heritage Center

OBERLIN, OHIO

*Small town, big story—
visit Oberlin, where
ordinary people have
done extraordinary things!*

Sarah Frances Gulick Jewett advocated fresh air, light, and exercise for healthy children over 100 years ago!

Founded in 1833, **Oberlin** quickly gained a reputation for being "different" when Oberlin College opened as the first co-educational college in the nation. Ever since, women in Oberlin have played crucial roles in the development of the town as artists, authors, graduates, philanthropists, educators, community leaders, and more.

DON'T MISS

- History of the first co-educational college in the nation
- Stories of the Underground Railroad
- Stilts and other games at the schoolhouse

FACILITIES

Visitors to the Oberlin Heritage Center tour three buildings. Within the Monroe House (1866), visitors hear stories about charity, the pursuit of education, and the history-altering struggles of women like Julia Monroe, Mary Elizabeth Johnston, and Lucy Stone. The Little Red Schoolhouse (1836) is a pioneer era school. One of the most notable pupils of Oberlin was Sarah Margru Kinson, a young African girl on the slave ship *Amistad* who later studied in Oberlin. In the Jewett House (1884) visitors learn about women's participation in reform movements, including Sarah

42

Frances Gulick Jewett who wrote popular health textbooks during the Progressive Era.

PROGRAMS

The Oberlin Heritage Center offers guided tours of its buildings, walking tours of historic downtown, and specialized tours for groups and schools. Public program topics include women's history, cultural diversity, historic preservation, and African and Native American history. Special programs include museum workshops, summer camps, and community-wide events. For more information, see events calendar and tour information at www.oberlinheritage.org.

COLLECTIONS

The Oberlin Heritage Center maintains genealogical files, oral histories, census records, city directories, photographs, object collections, and local building files in its Resource Center. It also has books about Oberlin, Oberlin College, women's history, and various local historical events. Interested scholars and community members are encouraged to arrange an appointment to use the Resource Center for research.

"A wife should no more take her husband's name than he should hers. My name is my identity and must not be lost."

– **Lucy Stone**, Oberlin graduate (1847) and women's rights advocate

Tours begin at the Monroe House, the beautifully restored home of community leaders James and Julia Monroe.

Oberlin Heritage Center
73½ South Professor Street
PO Box 455
Oberlin, OH 44074
440-774-1700
tourinfo@oberlinheritage.org
www.oberlinheritage.org

Check hours before visiting. Offices and Museum Store open Tuesday through Saturday 10 a.m. - 3 p.m. Guided tours Tuesday, Thursday, Saturday at 10:30 a.m., 1:30 p.m. Please check website for map and directions to parking area.

43

Maggie L. Walker National Historic Site

RICHMOND, VIRGINIA

Maggie L. Walker (1867-1934).

Home of Maggie L. Walker, first U.S. woman to charter a bank and become its president

As the Right Worthy Grand Secretary-Treasurer of the Independent Order of St. Luke, an African American fraternal organization, **Maggie L. Walker** started the St. Luke

Penny Savings Bank, the *St. Luke Herald* newspaper, and the St. Luke Emporium. Her quest for black economic independence provided a social network, professional jobs, and new opportunities for her people. By 1925, the Order had over 100,000 members in 24 states. A "womanist," Walker moved in the highest African American circles during the depths of Jim Crow segregation, lynchings, and pervasive denial of black Americans' rights.

FACILITIES

The Site includes the 1883 home she purchased in 1904, a visitor center, and exhibition building. Maggie L. Walker's two-story home, restored to its 1928 appearance, includes her

DON'T MISS

- Film on Maggie Walker's life and legacy
- Guided tour of Walker's elegant 28-room home with its 1928 elevator
- Junior Ranger Booklet—children can earn badges
- Independent Order of St. Luke buttons, sashes, and ritual books

extensive library with family diplomas and photographs of African Americans leaders, her ornate parlors, and her bedroom. The visitor center features her four-foot elaborate hall lamp with glass grapes that demonstrated her success, a film, and a bookstore on Walker, women's, African American, and Richmond history. Exhibits show Walker's life from impoverished childhood to nationally recognized accomplishments. A member of the NAACP National Board, she knew Mary McLeod Bethune, Nannie Helen Burroughs, W. E. B. DuBois, and many others.

PROGRAMS

Educational and interpretive programs present her life, family, activism, business contributions, and legacy. Visit the park website www.nps. gov/mawa for updates on special events. Call for tour

"Let us have a bank that will take the nickels and turn them into dollars."

— **Maggie L. Walker**

information and group reservations. All buildings and the home's first floor are wheelchair accessible. Free admission.

COLLECTIONS

The home features original furnishings she purchased and used. The 20,000 item collection includes Walker's multi-volume library, clothing, and personal effects as well as family artifacts, the Walker Family Papers, early 20th-century photographs, stereographs, sheet music, and Independent Order of St. Luke documents and ledgers.

Maggie L. Walker
National Historic Site
600 North 2nd Street
Richmond VA 23219
804-771-2017
www.nps.gov/mawa

Check hours before visiting.
Open Monday – Saturday seasonally from 9 a.m. – 4:30 p.m. beginning November 1, and 9:00 a.m. – 5:00 p.m. beginning March 1. Closed Thanksgiving, Christmas, and New Year's.

Maggie L. Walker's Richmond home managed by the National Park Service.

George Washington Birthplace National Monument

COLONIAL BEACH, VIRGINIA

NATIONAL PARK SERVICE

Where George Washington first slept

Setting the table at George Washington's birthplace.

George Washington was born here in 1732. Today, the National Park Service preserves the remaining 550 acres of the Washington family plantation at Popes Creek. He entered into an 18th-century British colonial

---

DON'T MISS

- Washington's 18th-century plantation landscape, where the Potomac River once connected to London markets
- Costumed interpreters working in the blacksmith shop, kitchen, and the farm
- Seeing, hearing, touching, and smelling the world that first shaped George Washington

world where tobacco was the dominant cash crop and colonial planters and their families worked with free, indentured, and enslaved labor. Although women in this society worked hard, society measured the success of free women by the achievements of their husbands, sons, and male relatives. George Washington's great-grandmother Ann Pope brought these lands to the Washington family. His mother, Mary Ball Washington, widowed with four young children, remained central to him throughout his life. These women and others of European, African, and Native American descent form unwritten chapters of the largely male history we know today.

FACILITIES

The Park has a visitor center with exhibits and a bookstore. The Memorial House is a 1930s replica of the birthplace. (The original house burned down in 1799.) Visitors tour the colonial farm, the Memorial House, the colonial kitchen, and the farm with barns, outbuildings, and heritage-breed farm animals. The Park contains the Washington family burial ground, the 17th-century archeological homesite, nature trails, and a picnic area.

PROGRAMS

Programs include exhibits, an introductory film, hourly guided costumed tours, and year-round special events.

"Truth will ultimately prevail where there is pains [sic] taken to bring it to light."

— **George Washington, 1794**

COLLECTIONS

The Park holds a collection of Washington commemorative items and memorabilia as well as Washington family items, including a Washington family Bible and tea table.

George Washington Birthplace
National Monument
1732 Popes Creek Road
Colonial Beach, VA 22443
804-732-1732
www.nps.gov/gewa

Check hours before visiting.
The Park is two miles off Virginia
Hwy 3, approximately 40 miles east
of Fredericksburg, VA.
The Park is open daily 9 a.m. - 5 p.m.

George Washington's original homesite.

Sewall-Belmont House & Museum

WASHINGTON, D.C.

Alice Paul toasting the Ratification Banner on August 18, 1920, the day Tennessee ratified the 19th Amendment, recognizing women's right to vote.

Celebrating the history of women's progress toward equality

Headquarters of the historic National Woman's Party (NWP), the **Sewall-Belmont House and Museum** was the Washington home of its founder and Equal Rights Amendment (ERA) author, activist, and lawyer Alice Paul. The Museum, named in the first Save America's Treasures legislation, is the only museum in the nation's capital dedicated to preserving and showcasing a crucial period in our history—the fight for American women's right to vote. The National Woman's Party fought for women's rights both in the United States and abroad. Suffragists picketed the White House, were arrested and imprisoned, and went on hunger strikes. Later, NWP members argued for inclusion of women in the 1964 Civil Rights Act.

DON'T MISS

- Suffragists Susan B. Anthony's desk, and Elizabeth Cady Stanton's chair
- Jailhouse Door pin awarded to imprisoned suffragists
- Nina Allender political cartoon collection

FACILITIES

The Sewall-Belmont House, built in 1800, is one of the oldest homes on Capitol Hill. Only a block from the U.S. Capitol, it has long been a center of political life and action in Washington, D.C.

PROGRAMS

The museum offers tours of the home/offices. Public programs showcase the legacy of NWP founder Alice Paul—the efforts towards women's equality—and share the untold and unfinished stories for the benefit of all the world's citizens.

COLLECTIONS

The National Woman's Party (NWP) collection provides an important resource for the study of the suffrage movement and the campaign for the Equal Rights Amendment. This unique collection, including the nation's first feminist library, documents the mass political movement for women's full citizenship in the 20th century, both in the United States and worldwide. The collection contains books, pamphlets, political cartoons, scrapbooks, photographs, records, newsletters, and artifacts produced by women and about women.

"May we not suggest Victory for Liberty in the United States?" by Nina Evans Allender, May 10, 1919.

Sewall-Belmont House & Museum

144 Constitution Avenue NE

Washington, DC 20002

202-546-1210

info@sewallbelmont.org

www.sewallbelmont.org

Check hours before visiting.
Open Wednesday - Sunday, 12 noon – 4 p.m. Tours offered at 12 noon, 1 p.m., 2 p.m., and 3 p.m.

The Sewall-Belmont House and Museum.

Mary McLeod Bethune Council House National Historic Site

WASHINGTON, D.C.

Mary McLeod Bethune (1876-1955).

The first headquarters of the National Council of Negro Women and home of the National Archives for Black Women's History

Mary McLeod Bethune was the 15th of 17 children of former slaves. She grew up amidst the poverty and oppression of the Reconstruction South yet rose to prominence as an educator, presidential advisor, and political activist. Her life demonstrated the value of education, a philosophy of universal love, and a wise and consistent use of political power in striving for racial and gender equality.

DON'T MISS

• Tour of the historic home and exhibits

FACILITIES

Mary McLeod Bethune achieved her greatest national and international recognition at this Washington, D.C., townhouse, the first headquarters of the National Council of Negro Women and her last home in Washington, D.C. From here, Bethune and the Council spearheaded strategies and developed programs that advanced the interests of African American women and the black community.

PROGRAMS

This National Historic Site offers visitors tours of the Council House, and special events and programs about the history of African American women.

50

COLLECTIONS

The Site maintains the Council House and its associated artifact collections, and is home to the National Archives for Black Women's History. The NABWH holds materials about Mrs. Bethune, the National Council of Negro Women, and other African American women's organizations and individuals. It also documents the ongoing Bethune legacy.

The first headquarters of the National Council of Negro Women at 1318 Vermont Avenue NW.

"I leave you love. I leave you hope. I leave you the challenge of developing confidence in one another. I leave you a thirst for education. I leave you respect for the uses of power. I leave you faith. I leave you racial dignity. I leave you a desire to live harmoniously with your fellow man. I leave you finally a responsibility to our young people."

— **Mary McLeod Bethune**

**Mary McLeod Bethune
Council House
National Historic Site
1318 Vermont Avenue NW
Washington, DC 20005-3607
202-673-2402
www.nps.gov/mamc**

Check hours before visiting.
Open year round Monday through
Saturday from 9 a.m. until 5 p.m.
The last tour starts at 4 p.m. Closed
Thanksgiving, Christmas, and New
Year's. The National Archives for
Black Women's History is open by
appointment only.

Frederick Douglass National Historic Site

WASHINGTON, D.C.

Frederick Douglass.

The **Frederick Douglass National Historic Site** preserves the life and legacy of one of the most famous—and amazing—19th-century African Americans (1818-1895), a runaway slave who became a diplomat and advisor to presidents. Editor, orator, organizer, official, and visionary, Douglass lived his beliefs. He worked to abolish slavery, to enfranchise everyone, and to promote the rights of oppressed people. His newspaper *The North Star* proclaimed "Right is of no Sex—Truth is of no Color." Active at the 1848 Women's Rights convention in Seneca Falls, New York, he signed its Declaration of Sentiments. Douglass knew John Brown, Abraham Lincoln, and Harriet Tubman. A lifelong women's rights activist, he died in 1895 just after addressing a Woman's Council meeting.

He was married 44 years to Anna Murray Douglass, a free black woman, who had helped him escape from slavery. After she died, he married Helen Pitts Douglass, a white woman, who helped save his home Cedar Hill by working with the National Association of Colored Women. Elizabeth Cady Stanton argued, "His lofty sentiments of liberty, justice and equality echoed on every platform over our broad land must influence and inspire many coming generations."

DON'T MISS

- Daily tours present his struggle to win equality for all people
- The website includes a virtual house tour, museum objects, photographs, and a lesson plan

FACILITIES

The Site includes a visitor center with exhibits and film on his life and times, bookstore, historic house museum, and eight-acre estate Cedar Hill including his "growlery." The 21-room mansion, with its furnishings and personal items, offers a rare opportunity to see the private side of this very public man. Here Douglass exercised with 12-pound dumbbells every morning and played his violin for his grandchildren at night. In his library, lined with over 800 books, he wrote his final autobiography, *The Life and Times of Frederick Douglass.*

Frederick Douglass's home.

PROGRAMS

Daily guided tours, annual events, interpretive talks, and living history programs. Events include an Annual Oratorical Contest where students present his speeches and address their meaning and power; a Civil Rights Film Festival featuring films that connect the "Father of the Civil Rights Movement" to the ongoing struggles for equal rights; and an annual Birthday Celebration, on February 14th, with civil rights activists and Oratorical Contest winners.

COLLECTIONS

The house's outstanding collection features over 8,000 objects, including Douglass's typewriter, bowler hat, laundry agitator, sewing machine, and family photographs. The collection clearly shows his connection to the abolitionist and women's rights movements; it includes a bust of his colleague Wendell Phillips and pictures of Elizabeth Cady Stanton and Susan B. Anthony.

**Frederick Douglass
National Historic Site
1411 W Street SE
Washington, DC 20020
www.nps.gov/frdo**

Please call or visit the website
for tour times and operating hours.
Reservations required for groups
larger than 11. Tour tickets available
in the visitor center.

53

General Federation of Women's Clubs

WASHINGTON, D.C.

GENERAL FEDERATION
of WOMEN'S CLUBS
www.GFWC.org

Headquarters, c. 1930.

International Headquarters of the General Federation of Women's Clubs and home of the GFWC Women's History and Resource Center

The General Federation of Women's Clubs (GFWC), an international organization of women volunteers founded in 1890, remains dedicated to volunteer service, community education, and women's empowerment. More than 100,000 members in the U.S. and worldwide work in their own communities to support the arts, preserve natural resources, advance education, promote healthy lifestyles, encourage civic involvement, and work toward world peace. GFWC has tackled important American issues: women's suffrage, child labor, juvenile court laws, the Pure Food and Drug Act, the establishment of national parks, the presservation of Native American culture, peacetime uses of technology, libraries and literacy, wartime civil service, domestic violence, the establishment of the

---

DON'T MISS

- Albert Herter murals
- Herschede tall case clock with unique Canterbury chime
- Suffragist Lucretia Mott's bonnet
- Archival documents on notable GFWC clubwomen, including Julia Ward Howe, Jane Addams, and Eleanor Roosevelt

United Nations, and the Equal Rights Amendment.

FACILITIES

In 1922, the GFWC purchased its headquarters, a splendid Victorian (1875) townhouse filled with unique architectural details, art, and artifacts. Now a National Historic Landmark in the Dupont Circle neighborhood, the building also houses the Women's History and Resource Center (WHRC) that preserves and makes the GFWC's historic collections accessible.

PROGRAMS

GFWC headquarters offers visitors tours, special events, exhibits related to GFWC programs and collections, and WHRC research. With advanced notice, staff will provide small groups with customized, hands-on "experience" tours.

COLLECTIONS

GFWC collections document the social and political contributions of GFWC clubwomen through its extensive archives, related special collections, publications, and its historic furnishings, art, and artifacts. Exhibits highlight GFWC's collection of regional art, unique arts and crafts, panoramic photographs, and GFWC

"We look for unity, but unity in diversity."

— **Ella Dietz Clymer, 1889**

Music room.

memorabilia (pins, badges, and gavels). A special exhibit illustrating GFWC's role in promoting the appreciation of American art features color woodblock prints of Helen Hyde and Gustave Baumann.

General Federation of Women's Clubs Headquarters and Women's History and Resource Center 1734 N Street NW Washington, DC 20036-2990 202-347-3168 www.GFWC.org

Check hours before visiting.
Open Monday – Friday, 9 a.m. - 4 p.m.
Closed on all federal holidays and from Christmas Eve through New Year's.
Tours and research by appointment.

Clara Barton National Historic Site

GLEN ECHO, MARYLAND

Clara Barton (1821-1912).

Clara Barton's home and headquarters of the American Red Cross

Clara Barton was a remarkable person. As a young woman, she taught school in Massachusetts and New Jersey and worked as a clerk at the Patent Office in Washington, D.C. But she gained fame as a Civil War battlefield nurse. In 1881, she founded the American Red Cross and served as its president for 23 years. Her Glen Echo home served as the American Red Cross head-

quarters and warehouse, and her living quarters for her and staff between 1897 and 1904. Everything about the place conveys her sense of duty, commitment, and dedication to serving others.

FACILITIES

The National Park Service has restored 11 rooms, including the 1897 American Red Cross National Headquarters offices and Clara Barton's private bedroom. The tour includes three levels; only the first floor is wheelchair accessible. A small bookstore includes materials related to Clara Barton and titles on women's history and the Victorian Era. There are two Eastern National "Passport to Your National Parks" imprint stamps available. Glen Echo Park is adjacent. Free admission.

DON'T MISS

- "Bandage material" ceilings
- Hidden closets filled with relief supplies
- Center hallway with open air well
- Painting of Tommy, Clara Barton's cat

56

PROGRAMS

Guided tours, special exhibits, and special programs are conducted year round. A Junior Ranger program is available and includes Glen Echo Park. Hands-on interactive tours for school or children's groups or groups of ten or more require reservations. An on-line virtual tour and interactive school/Junior Ranger program is available on the website www.nps.gov/clba.

COLLECTIONS

This is not the typical Victorian house museum. A wonderful blend of period pieces, mixed with Clara Barton's original possessions, truly gives visitors a sense of her home as she knew it. The main restoration period is 1897–1904. Restored American Red Cross offices display period typewriters, a graphophone, and telephone. The bed where Clara Barton died in 1912 is also featured on the tour.

"Mine has not been the kind of work usually given to women to perform, and no man can quite comprehend the situation. No man is ever called to do a man's work with only a woman's power and surroundings. How can he comprehend it?"

– **Clara Barton**

Red Cross pattern in stained glass windows.

Clara Barton
National Historic Site
5801 Oxford Road
Glen Echo, MD 20812
301-320-1410
www.nps.gov/clba

Check hours before visiting. Open year-round, daily, except January 1, Thanksgiving Day, and December 25. Guided tours on the hour 10 a.m. – 4 p.m. Administered by the George Washington Memorial Parkway.

Clara Barton National Historic Site.

Paulsdale National Historic Landmark

MOUNT LAUREL,
NEW JERSEY

Honoring Alice Paul's legacy, preserving her home, developing future leaders

Alice Paul, c. 1900.

The **Alice Paul Institute** is a non-profit organization dedicated to educating the public about the life and work of New Jersey's most famous suffragist, Alice Stokes Paul (1885-1977), champion of women's voting rights, author of the Equal Rights Amendment (in 1923), founder of the National Woman's Party, and a lifelong activist for women's equality. API's mission is to educate the public about her life, preserve historic Paulsdale, develop future leaders, and work towards achieving women's equality.

FACILITIES

The exterior and interior of Paulsdale have been restored to their appearance during Alice Paul's residence (1885-1920). The 200-year-old farmhouse stands on 6.5 acres of property. The home features a wrap-around porch, kitchen, double parlor, and dining room (API's gift shop). Modern amenities include a handicapped accessible bathroom, small staging kitchen, and handicapped access to the

DON'T MISS

- Alice Paul's six college degrees
- Her parent's 1881 Quaker marriage certificate
- Her mid-19th-century bookcase
- The Paul family tree

first floor. API offices occupy the second floor.

PROGRAMS

API offers a variety of programs through the Alice Paul Leadership Program and API Heritage Program. Educational programs include G.O.L.D. (Girls Overnight Leadership Development); Meeting Alice, a fourth-grade history field-trip program; Celebrate New Jersey Women, a history-based program for Girl Scouts; and Girlblazers Summer Camp, a two-week camp utilizing female role-models to teach girls leadership skills. API also offers a variety of heritage events for adults, including presentations, films, teas, tours, and workshops.

COLLECTIONS

The Alice Paul Archives are available for public research by appointment. The collection includes original *The Suffragist* and *Equal Rights* newspapers,

Paulsdale.

"I never doubted that equal rights was the right direction. Most reforms, most problems are complicated. But to me there is nothing complicated about ordinary equality."

— **Alice Paul**

photographs, and Alice Paul's personal book collection. Researchers are also welcome to visit and borrow from the API Women's History Library, a growing collection of books on Alice Paul, suffrage, New Jersey history, and women's history.

Alice Paul Institute
128 Hooton Road
PO Box 1376 (mailing address)
Mount Laurel, NJ 08054
856-231-1885
Fax 856-231-4223
info@alicepaul.org
www.alicepaul.org

Visit website for tour dates, upcoming events, ways to support API, and additional information on Alice Paul and the Alice Paul Institute.

Pearl S. Buck House National Historic Landmark

PERKASIE, PENNSYLVANIA

Pearl S. Buck
HOUSE

Opening Doors to a Cross-Cultural Legacy

Portrait of Pearl S. Buck.

The Pearl S. Buck House promotes the legacy of award-winning author and humanitarian, Pearl S. Buck, through interpretive tours of her home and programs that develop cross-cultural understanding and build worldwide partnerships

Nobel Prize winning **Pearl S. Buck** once lived and wrote here. Situated on a picturesque 68-acre estate with flagstone walkways, this circa 1820s stone farmhouse

retains a fully-intact collection of her belongings and an assortment of original paintings by renowned artists. On display is the famed desk where she wrote *The Good Earth* (1931), the Pulitzer Prize winning novel of Chinese village life that profoundly influenced American attitudes about China.

FACILITIES

An excellent example of 19th-century architecture, the Pearl S. Buck home has greenhouses, a cottage, a milk house, and an 1827 renovated barn that houses the international gift shop and cultural center. Magnificent rolling hills, tranquil ponds, and glorious perennial gardens surround the house. The site is handicapped-accessible, and

DON'T MISS

- International gift shop and online marketplace

60

buses are welcome. Picnic areas, ample parking, and rental space are available all year for meetings, weddings, receptions, and parties, including Garden Tent (300 people max).

PROGRAMS

Changing exhibits convey aspects of Pearl S. Buck's life in-depth. For tour times, group discounts, or other inquiries, call or visit the website. School tours offered include interdisciplinary tours with connections in liter-ature, social studies, geography, Pennsylvania history, and more. All school tours include a guided house tour, a grounds visit, and a visit to the gift shop.

COLLECTIONS

The fully-intact collection reflects Pearl Buck's multicultural life. The home's furnishings, artwork, and personal belongings from both the Dalai Lama and

Pearl S. Buck House.

"You fall in love with a house just as you do a person."

– Pearl S. Buck

The Good Earth Desk in Library of the Pearl S. Buck House.

President Nixon are on display. An electronically-catalogued archival collection of original Pearl Buck documents is an invaluable resource for research-ers, scholars, and curators.

Pearl S. Buck House
& Historic Site
520 Dublin Road
Perkasie, PA 18944
215-249-0100
www.pearlsbuck.org

Check hours before visiting. Open March-December; closed January and February. Guided tours: Tuesday - Saturday 11 a.m., 1 p.m., and 2 p.m. Sunday 1 p.m. and 2 p.m. Closed Mondays and holidays. Reservations not needed; requested for groups of 10 or more.

American Swedish Historical Museum

PHILADELPHIA, PENNSYLVANIA

A place where people of all nationalities who enjoy Swedish architecture, art, history, and tradition come together

The American Swedish Historical Museum seeks to create awareness in America of the contributions of Swedish culture. This Museum collects, preserves, exhibits, publishes, and interprets the history of

---

DON'T MISS

Galleries showcasing three famous 19th-century Swedish women:
- Soprano "Swedish Nightingale" Jenny Lind
- Feminist, novelist, and traveler Fredrika Bremer
- 1909 Nobel Prize winner in Literature Selma Lagerlöf

Portrait bust of the Swedish soprano Jenny Lind at the American Swedish Historical Museum.

Swedish and Swedish American women and men, with a concentration on the New Sweden colonial period (1638-1655) in now-Delaware and Pennsylvania.

FACILITIES

The museum building reflects both Swedish and American architectural elements. The Swedish inspiration comes from a 17th-century manor house; the copper cupola is a copy of one on top of Stockholm's City Hall. The American influence is represented by the exterior galleries, created in a variety of

arcades, modeled after Mount Vernon. There are 12 permanent styles ranging from art-deco to international, as well as an extensive research library.

PROGRAMS

The Museum celebrates the richness of the Swedish and Swedish American cultural heritage with annual events and traditional holiday observances, such as *Luciafest,* Crayfish Party, *Valborgsmässoafton,* and *Midsommarfest.* Language classes, cooking classes, exhibitions, concerts, and lectures also present learning opportunities year round. Educational programs serve all ages: field trips for preschoolers feature the fictional girl Pippi Longstocking; annual scholarly New Sweden History Conferences explore new research into the early Swedish settlement.

COLLECTIONS

Special exhibitions feature contemporary art, or cultural or historical topics. The permanent collection includes three galleries devoted to the history of the New Sweden Colony established in the Delaware Valley in 1638. Other galleries concentrate on more recent history, including Alfred Nobel and the Nobel Prizes. An

The Grand Hall of the American Swedish Historical Museum in Philadelphia.

interior of a Swedish *stuga,* or one-room farmhouse, honors the large wave of Swedish immigration to America during the second half of the 1800s.

American Swedish Historical Museum
1900 Pattison Avenue
Philadelphia, PA 19145
215-389-1776
www.americanswedish.org

Check hours before visiting.
Open Tuesday - Friday 10 a.m. - 4 p.m.;
weekends 12 noon - 4 p.m.

New Century Trust

PHILADELPHIA, PENNSYLVANIA

Improving the lives of Philadelphia area women and girls

The New Century Trust purchased this 10,000-square-foot residence in 1903 and converted it into a building that accommodated its many activities.

The **New Century Trust** traces its roots to the Women's Pavilion at the 1876 Centennial Exposition held in Philadelphia. In 1882, Eliza Sproat Turner (1826-1903), a progressive thinker and wealthy activist, founded the New Century Guild for Working Women to

---

DON'T MISS

- Kimberly Clark's dramatic Women in History mural

Eliza Sproat Turner, 1898. Oil portrait by Cecilia Beaux commissioned to honor Turner's leadership in founding the New Century Guild in 1882 and the NCT in 1893.

assist young women flocking to the city for jobs. In 1893, the New Century Trust became the incorporated body of the earlier Guild.

OVERVIEW

Activities in the Trust's early history included classes and lectures for working women and girls; "Noon Rest," a dining room where hundreds of working women had a hot meal and rest during their lunch break; temporary lodging; and emergency financial support. The Trust sponsored *The Working Woman's Journal,* a nationally circulated publication dealing with workforce issues, actively supporting women's suffrage and the consumer rights movement.

One of the earliest, largest, and most successful of many similar organizations created during the 19th century, The New Century Trust is also one of the most long-lived. Today, the Trust continues its founders' philanthropic mission by making grants to non-profit organizations to improve the lives of Philadelphia-area women and girls. The Trust also preserves and interprets its landmark building.

FACILITIES

Located in downtown Philadelphia, The New Century Trust does not have regular public hours. Interested visitors must call and make advance arrangements for tours. The Trust's archives are housed at the Historical Society of Pennsylvania. A large mural on the west side of the building honors women's history and the work of The New Century Trust and its former committee, the New Century Guild.

New Century Trust
1307 Locust Street
Philadelphia, PA 19107
215-735-7593
newcenturytrust@verizon.net

Open to visitors by arrangement only.

Women in History Mural by Kimberly Clark. 2001; paint on stucco.

Independence National Historical Park

PHILADELPHIA, PENNSYLVANIA

Martha Washington.

Tells the story of the men and women involved in the founding and growth of the United States of America (1776-1836)

War and independence affected women deeply. **Independence Hall,** the Liberty Bell Center, Franklin Court, and Dolley Todd Madison's house are just four of 24 park sites associated with this country's founding years, telling the story of the women behind the "founding fathers." The Liberty Bell Center discusses the symbolic use of the Liberty Bell by abolitionists such as Lucretia Mott and by the woman suffrage movement. The Second Bank's Portrait Gallery features women's portraits, including Martha Washington and Dolley Todd Madison. Franklin Court highlights the crucial role that Benjamin Franklin's wife Deborah Franklin played during his long absences in building their house, overseeing his business, and defending her home from an anti-Stamp Tax mob.

DON'T MISS

- The Visitor Center's Revolutionary Era girl's tea set and wooden doll, and women's toothbrushes and hair combs
- The Portrait Gallery's paintings of notable women
- The "middling" Todd and upper-class Bishop White house tours

66

The women in President Washington's household, including his wife Martha and enslaved African seamstress Ona Judge, are discussed at the nearby Germantown White House and the new President's House Site Commemoration (opening 2010). In 1796, with the help of Philadelphia's large free black population, Judge seized her freedom and escaped to New Hampshire. She married there, raised a family, and eluded Washington's several efforts to get her back.

The Liberty Bell with Independence Hall beyond. Photograph by Robin Miller.

PROGRAMS

Park tours include: the Todd House, where young Dolley Todd lived before her husband died in the 1793 yellow fever epidemic (she later married future President James Madison); and the Bishop William White House, which features his wife Mary, housekeeper Mrs. Boggs, and servants who slept in its attic and worked in its basement. In addition, a program discusses the women's suffrage movement and the Liberty Bell. The Junior Ranger booklet features an 18th-century girl "Mattie."

Independence NHP
143 South 3rd Street
Philadelphia, PA 19106
800-537-7676
www.nps.gov/inde

Check hours before visiting. Open daily 9 a.m. – 5 p.m., except Christmas Day for Independence Hall and the Liberty Bell. Programs and building hours vary seasonally—call or check park website. Start at the Visitor Center at 525 Market Street.

dining parlor in the Dolley Todd House. urtesy of Top Gun Photographers.

The Nathaniel Newlin Grist Mill

GLEN MILLS, PENNSYLVANIA

Preserving our cultural and environmental heritage

The Miller's House kitchen.

First established in 1704 by Quakers Nathaniel and Mary Mendenhall Newlin, the **Newlin Grist Mill** operated until 1941, grinding wheat, corn, oats, buckwheat, and rye for the growing Mid-Atlantic colony. In 1958, Elizabeth and Mortimer Newlin created a foundation to preserve their ancestor's accomplishments. Elizabeth Newlin recognized the integral part women played in colonial life. She painstakingly gathered a collection of decorative arts for the Miller's House, thus showing colonial women's stories. Newlin's love of nature and promotion of conservation preserved the open space that now surrounds the grist mill.

FACILITIES

The Newlin Foundation manages 12 historic structures and 160 acres with trails through wetlands, forest, and grasslands. Buildings open for visitor tours include the 1704 gristmill, 1739 Miller's House, blacksmith shop, and Markham Railroad Station. Other remaining buildings include the 1739 Trimble House,

DON'T MISS

- Working colonial grist mill
- Elizabeth Newlin's collection of lighting devices
- Hiking trails and beautiful Sequoia and Dawn Redwood trees

spring house, 1790s barn, bake oven, and various outbuildings.

PROGRAMS

Tours, school programs, demonstrations, and special events explore the "Mill as Nexus." As the center of its community, the mill interprets late 17th- to early 18th-century Mid-Atlantic agriculture, technology, trade, and nearby peoples' lives. Environmental programs include nature walks for students, Summer Discovery Camp, and a series titled "Bird Walks and Nature Talks."

COLLECTIONS

The Newlin Grist Mill's collections consist of milling-related objects and late 17th- to early 18th-century decorative arts. Elizabeth Newlin's collection of decorative arts, kitchen equipment, textiles, and lighting devices show daily life in rural southeastern Pennsylvania. The H. Dabbs Woodfin Research Archive houses materials related to the Newlin family, milling in the upper Delaware Valley, and local history.

The Nathaniel Newlin Grist Mill

219 South Cheyney Road

Glen Mills, PA 19342

610-459-2359

info@newlingristmill.org

www.newlingristmill.org

Open 9 a.m. – 4 p.m. daily, year round. Check hours before visiting.

Newlin Miller's House.

Eleanor Roosevelt National Historic Site

HYDE PARK, NEW YORK

Eleanor Roosevelt (1884-1962).

Val-Kill, the home of a First Lady (wife of President Franklin Delano Roosevelt), an influential social and political 20th-century activist

Eleanor Roosevelt fought for racial and gender equality, social and economic justice, and world peace. She transcended her era's upper-class expectations that marriage, family, and charity work be the focus of a woman's life, becoming America's conscience and a political force. She chaired the United Nation's Human Rights Commission and led in the creation of the Universal Declaration of Human Rights.

FACILITIES

The Site includes Eleanor Roosevelt's home and grounds, a visitor center with exhibits, and a fair trade museum shop.

PROGRAMS

The Park has an introductory film and guided tour of the place that Eleanor Roosevelt called home. Tours through her home showcase her use of Val-Kill as a place to further her work in social and

DON'T MISS

- New exhibits on her activism
- The desk where she wrote her "My Day" column, books, and articles, and personally answered letters
- The hiking trail she enjoyed daily

economic justice, political activism, and the Universal Declaration of Human Rights. Winston Churchill, future President John F. Kennedy, and Katherine Hepburn visited her here. Issues Mrs. Roosevelt discussed with guests or through her writings show the relevancy of her ideas to today's world. Education programs are available by advanced reservation.

Val-Kill, Eleanor Roosevelt's home.

COLLECTIONS

Eleanor Roosevelt's home contains colonial reproduction furniture and pewter produced at the Val-Kill Furniture Factory, opened to provide jobs for local farm youth during a time when people were migrating to cities seeking jobs. Documentary materials and artifacts from her life (silver nut dishes, a porcelain

Eleanor Roosevelt's office at Val-Kill.

Eleanor Roosevelt's suitcase.

tape dispenser, and a tattered suitcase carried on her many trips) are located at the Franklin D. Roosevelt Presidential Library Museum, two miles away.

Eleanor Roosevelt
National Historic Site
Route 9-G
Hyde Park, NY 12538
845-229-9422 or 9115
www.nps.gov/elro

Check hours before visiting.
Open 9 a.m. - 5 p.m., May through October, 7 days per week; 1 p.m. - 4 p.m., November through April, Thursday through Monday.

Martin Van Buren National Historic Site

KINDERHOOK, NEW YORK

The only known image of President Martin Van Buren's wife Hannah.

Lindenwald, the home and farm of eighth President of the U.S., Martin Van Buren

Although the **Martin Van Buren National Historic Site** initially appears to be a traditional house museum dedicated to a male patriarch, a closer looks reveals a wealth of women's history. Many women lived there, including Lindenwald's Irish domestic

---

DON'T MISS

- Personal effects of the female servant's lives, such as a porcelain dog given as a gift by the president, or the Roman Catholic rosary beads hanging on the bedpost

workers, its Southern belle hostess Angelica Singleton Van Buren, and Van Buren's niece, Christina Cantine, a reform-oriented woman from the "burned over district" of western New York. All these people are indispensable to telling the whole story of Martin Van Buren's life after his presidency.

Lindenwald illustrates American society's changes in the 1840s and 1850s, from kitchen technology (a coal burning stove and hand operated water pump) to greater political male participation and female organization; from lonely single Irish immigrant women to Northern women gaining greater marital and property rights as their Southern sisters' rights remained quite limited. The women of this presidential farm and retirement home illustrate the diverse lives—and conflicts—experienced by American women. When enlarged and transformed into an Italianate showplace, Lindenwald segregated its "family" from its "workers," physically as well as socially.

PROGRAMS

Lindenwald features a tour of the home's basement work areas to illuminate its domestic workers' lives.

COLLECTIONS

Artifacts include a servant's call bell used to summon the Irish women servants, often young immigrants fleeing the 1840s

Lindenwald's formal parlor, with its upholstered furniture and Brussels carpets, shows a genteel way of life supported by an enormous amount of housework.

Irish famine, as well as a cameo of Hannah Van Buren, the only known image of Van Buren's wife, who died in 1819, long before her husband became president. He never remarried.

Martin Van Buren
National Historic Site
1013 Old Post Road
Kinderhook, NY 12106
518-758-9689
www.nps.gov/mava

Check hours before visiting.
Open for tours daily, May through October.

Lindenwald was the centerpiece of a large community that reflected the diversity of mid-19th-century rural life and work in the Hudson Valley.

Kate Mullany National Historic Site

TROY, NEW YORK

Kate Mullany House.

Home of the American Labor Studies Center

In February 1864, **Kate Mullany** and her co-worker Esther Keegan organized some 300 women into the first female union in America—the Troy Collar Laundry Union in Troy, New York. Shortly after forming the union, the women went on strike from 14 commercial laundry establishments demanding a 25% wage increase and improved working conditions. For nearly six days, the new union members stayed away from their jobs. The employers granted their demands.

DON'T MISS

- Visit website for restoration update news

In 1868, William Sylvis appointed Mullany assistant secretary of the National Labor Union, the first time a woman was appointed to a national labor union office. In 1864, her mother Bridgit purchased land at 350 Eighth Street in Troy, where Mullany built a family residence and income-producing property in 1869.

FACILITIES

The Mullany House is currently undergoing renovation and restoration, with plans to restore the third-floor Mullany apartment and historic stairwell to its 1869 configuration. The first floor houses an exhibit area; the second floor, offices of the American Labor Studies Center. Kate Mullany Park, honoring trade union women pioneers, will be developed on adjacent property. The site will open to the public when the restoration and furnishing of the apartment are completed.

PROGRAMS

The Kate Mullany House is home to the American Labor Studies Center (ALSC), which promotes the integration of labor history into the K-12 curriculum nationwide. Under a grant from the National Park Service, the ALSC is developing standards-based lessons on Kate Mullany and the Troy Collar Laundry Union. Plans are underway to develop education and interpretive programs with special emphasis on K-12 students, once the property is open to the public.

"We now have a recognized officer from the female side of the house—one of the smartest and most energetic women in America."

– **William H. Sylvis,** President
National Labor Union, 1868

Kate Mullany
National Historic Site
350 Eighth Street
Troy, NY 12180
Mail: 16 Birchwood Court
Loudonville, NY 12211
518-331-4474
paulfcole@aol.com
www.katemullanynhs.org
www.labor-studies.org

First Lady Hillary Rodham Clinton (right) at the Mullany House NHL dedication.

Women's Rights National Historical Park

SENECA FALLS AND WATERLOO, NEW YORK

"The center of the rebellion"

The "First Wave" Statue grouping at the park visitor center depicts participants in the first women's rights convention, held in Seneca Falls in 1848.

In 1848, four Quaker women joined Elizabeth Cady Stanton in inviting the public to the **First Women's Rights Convention** to discuss expanding the role, and rights, of women in America. At the end of the two days, 100 people made a public commitment to work together to improve women's quality of life. Stanton called the convention, which launched a national movement for women's rights, "a grand success." While women have achieved greater equality with the vote, property rights, and education, the revolution continues today.

DON'T MISS

- Wesleyan Methodist Chapel, 1848 site of the nation's first women's rights convention
- Visitor center and award-winning film, *Dreams of Equality*
- The Seneca-Cayuga Canal in Downtown Seneca Falls and Waterloo
- Seasonally: Elizabeth Cady Stanton Home and M'Clintock House

FACILITIES

Elizabeth Cady Stanton's home, which she called "the center of the rebellion" for women's rights, and the M'Clintock house, the Waterloo nexus of a national anti-slavery network, are open seasonally. The Wesleyan Methodist Chapel and visitor center are open year round. The Women's Rights National Historical Park is part of the National Underground Railroad Network to Freedom and the Erie Canalway National Heritage Corridor, and two New York State heritage trails.

PROGRAMS

Exhibits, film, ranger-led tours, educational programs, and special programs are available.

COLLECTIONS

Materials related to Elizabeth Cady Stanton and to the families of the 100 signers of the Declaration of Sentiments are available to researchers by appointment.

" . . . all men and women are created equal . . ."
– Declaration of Sentiments, 1848

Elizabeth Cady Stanton House.

Women's Rights National Historical Park
136 Fall Street
Seneca Falls, NY 13148
315-568-0024
Fax 315-568-2141
wori_information_desk@
nps.gov
www.nps.gov/wori

Check hours before visiting.
Open 9 a.m. - 5 p.m. Open year
round except some winter holidays.

Wesleyan Methodist Chapel.

1816 Farmington Quaker Meetinghouse

FARMINGTON, NEW YORK

Farmington echoes debates on woman's rights, Seneca Indians, and the Underground Railroad

Quaker minister Lucretia Mott often spoke in the Farmington Meetinghouse. Courtesy of Friends Historical Society, Swarthmore College.

As a crucible of major American reform movements, the 1816 **Farmington Quaker Meetinghouse** tells the story of debates over freedom and equality for women, Seneca Indians, and African Americans in upstate New York and the nation. Famous Americans associated with Farmington include Lucretia Mott, Frederick Douglass, Austin Steward, William Wells Brown, Elizabeth Cady Stanton, and Susan B. Anthony.

of the colonial settlement area in North America. Twenty-five Quaker meetings from all over western New York, Ontario, and Michigan originated from Farmington meeting.

FACILITY

This meetinghouse, perhaps the largest pre-canal building in central and western New York, is one of the earliest known Quaker meetinghouses still standing west

1816 Quaker Meetinghouse. Courtesy of Macedon Town Historian.

HISTORY

The 1816 Farmington Quaker Meetinghouse was a center for national debates about woman's rights. At least one-quarter of the signers of the Declaration of Sentiments at the first woman's rights convention at Seneca Falls in July 1848 attended Farmington Quarterly meeting. Lucretia Mott spoke often in this Meetinghouse. Elizabeth Cady Stanton spoke here in October 1848, and Susan B. Anthony spoke here in 1873 at the time of her trial for voting.

The Meetinghouse became the focus of a community restoration project after a February 2006 storm.

Interior of Meetinghouse. Courtesy of Friends Historical Society, Swarthmore College.

The 1816 Farmington Quaker Meetinghouse represents the historic relationship of mutual respect between Quakers and Native Americans. In 1838, Senecas and Quakers met at this meetinghouse to prevent loss of Seneca lands and a "trail of tears." It also honors Farmington as a nationally important Underground Railroad center. Dozens, and perhaps hundreds, of freedom seekers, linked to a network that extended into Maryland, Delaware, and Washington, D.C., came through Farmington. Contributions for restoring the Meetinghouse may be sent to the 1816 Farmington Quaker Meetinghouse, c/o Elizabeth Cady Stanton Foundation, PO Box 603, Seneca Falls, NY 13148.

**Farmington Quaker
Meetinghouse
160 County Route 8
Farmington, NY
www.farmingtonmeetinghouse.org**

Not currently open to the public.

The Matilda Joslyn Gage Home

FAYETTEVILLE, NEW YORK

The Matilda Joslyn Gage Foundation℠

DARE TO SEEK JUSTICE

Matilda Joslyn Gage.

The historic home of Matilda Joslyn Gage

Matilda Joslyn Gage (1826-1898), a women's rights advocate and an abolitionist, was also the mother-in-law of L. Frank Baum, author of *The Wizard of Oz*. Her Fayetteville home is part of the New York State Underground Railroad Heritage Trail and the federal Votes for Women and Network to Freedom trails. Now undergoing an extensive rehabilitation, the home will be open to the public in 2010.

DON'T MISS

- The room where layers of wallpaper have been stripped away to reveal the pattern visible when Gage lived there
- The Susan B. Anthony window, where her name is etched in the glass
- Artifacts unearthed by archeological digs on the property

FACILITIES

A set of 1887 photos is guiding the Gage Home rehabilitation project. The Matilda Joslyn Gage Foundation owns and operates the Greek revival home along with a nearby building that houses administrative offices, a gift shop, and a library of feminism. The Gage Home is part of Fayetteville's historic district, which dates from the era when Fayetteville was a bustling Erie Canal village.

PROGRAMS

The home is currently open for scheduled tours and by appointment. Visitors can enjoy tea and see the rehabilitation work in process. Walking tours of Gage's Fayetteville and of the village's historic cemetery are also available. The Gage Home offers programming in five areas related to Gage's life and the theme Conscience in Community: women's rights, the Haudenosaunee (Iroquois) influence, the Underground Railroad, Oz, and religious freedom.

"There is a word sweeter than Mother, Home, or Heaven. That word is Liberty."

– Matilda Joslyn Gage,
the words carved on her tombstone
in the Fayetteville cemetery

COLLECTIONS

Collections include Gage Family furnishings and memorabilia; archives containing letters, journals, genealogical records, and other writings; and an extensive collection of photographs, including some taken by L. Frank Baum.

The Matilda Joslyn Gage Foundation
PO Box 192
109 Walnut Street
Fayetteville, NY 13066
Phone/Fax 315-637-9511
Foundation@MatildaJoslyn
Gage.org
www.MatildaJoslynGage.org

Check hours before visiting.
Office open Monday - Friday 9:30 - 5 p.m.
Call ahead for tours.

The Gage Home at 210 East Genesee Street in Fayetteville, Central New York.

The Harriet Beecher Stowe Center

HARTFORD, CONNECTICUT

STOWE CENTER
HARRIET BEECHER
The Harriet Beecher Stowe House and Library

The gardens and historic home of one of the nation's most influential authors

Harriet Beecher Stowe.

Harriet Beecher Stowe (1811-1896) published more than 30 books. Her best selling novel, *Uncle Tom's Cabin*, galvanized the Anti-Slavery movement and turned Stowe into an international celebrity. Stowe was the middle child of the influential Beecher family that included her sisters, education reformer Catharine Beecher and women's rights activist Isabella Beecher Hooker. Stowe's final home, located in Hartford, Connecticut, is the heart of the Harriet Beecher Stowe Center.

DON'T MISS

- Beautiful Victorian-style gardens
- Stowe's artwork
- Exceptional museum store
- The Stowe Center Research Library
- Special exhibitions

FACILITIES

The Stowe Center site includes ove
two acres of Victorian gardens and
grounds and three buildings:
Stowe's 1871 home, its kitchen

based on ideals published in *The American Woman's Home* (1869) co-authored by Stowe and sister Catharine Beecher; the 1884 Katharine Seymour Day House, with the Center's research library and administrative offices; and the 1873 visitor center and museum shop.

PROGRAMS

Through public, thematic tours, school programs, Teachers' Institutes, and special events, the Stowe Center tells the stories of this influential family and the important roles they played in 19th-century U.S. history. It inspires individuals to embrace Stowe's commitment to social justice.

COLLECTIONS

The Harriet Beecher Stowe Center holds the world's most extensive

The Harriet Beecher Stowe Center is open year round.

Harriet Beecher Stowe— Her words changed the world.

collection of manuscripts and materials related to the life and works of the extended Beecher/ Stowe family. The house is filled with family furnishings, revealing the Beecher/Stowe influence in domestic interiors. The library contains over 200,000 items, including material on women's rights and African-American history. For specialized collection research, contact the Curator or Collection Manager.

The Harriet Beecher Stowe Center
77 Forest Street
Hartford, CT 06105
860-522-9258
Fax 860-522-9259
info@StoweCenter.org
www.harrietbeecherstowe.org

Check hours before visiting. Open year round. Wednesday – Saturday : 9:30-4:30 p.m. Sunday: Noon – 4:30 p.m. Tuesdays: June-October 9:30 – 4:30 p.m. CLOSED: Every Monday and January 1, Easter Sunday, July 4, Thanksgiving, December 24-25. Library open by appointment only.

Springfield Armory National Historic Site

SPRINGFIELD, MASSACHUSETTS

World War II poster honoring Women Ordnance Workers.

The Armory hired women starting with World War I and greatly expanded their employment during World War II

For nearly two centuries, until it closed in 1968, **Springfield Armory** workers developed, tested, manufactured, repaired, and stored U.S. Army rifles and small arms. Methods developed here at the armory stimulated technological innovation, improved manufacturing processes, and increased the use of labor-saving machines throughout American industry. In the 20th century, increasing numbers of women and African Americans worked in the Armory shaping steel and wooden components of military rifles and assembling the finished weapons. During World War II, nearly 42% of the over 14,000 Armory workers were women, up from 15% in World War I. Women were crucial to these war efforts, filling workforce shortages as men left for military service.

DON'T MISS

- "Organ of Muskets"–Civil War double rifle musket rack
- Blanchard lathe gunstock shaping machine
- Great Tower spiral staircase
- Lyle life-saving gun to shoot lifelines out to wrecked ships

FACILITIES

Today, Springfield Armory National Historic Site preserves and interprets this colorful history in original buildings on their historic grounds through museum displays, public programs, notable collections, activities, and internet resources. The visitor center has an Eastern National bookstore (www.eparks.com).

PROGRAMS

Programs present many people and events in this richly multi-layered place that influenced our nation's history. The Museum offers oral history recordings of men and women workers, recreated Women Ordnance Worker (WOW) programs for students, and, at the bookstore, "Rosie the Riveter" materials.

"It was Pearl Harbor in 1941 and they said, 'Why don't you go over to the Springfield Armory, they're hiring like crazy over there.'"

– Lillian LaBranch Duffy

COLLECTIONS

This park has the world's most extensive collection of historic U.S. military firearms, many viewed in the museum alongside industrial history exhibits, as well as an archive of over 100,000 documents and images detailing the nearly two centuries of the Springfield Armory operations as the longest continuously operated industrial site in the U.S.

Building 13 Langone 2006.

Springfield Armory
National Historic Site
One Armory Square, Suite 2
Springfield, MA 01105
413-734-8551
www.nps.gov/spar

Check hours before visiting.
Open seven days per week, 9 a.m. -
5 p.m., except Thanksgiving,
Christmas, & New Year's.
Directions: www.nps.gov/spar/plan
yourvisit/directions.htm

Minute Man National Historical Park

CONCORD,
MASSACHUSETTS

Louisa May Alcott (1832-1888).
Photograph courtesy of the NPS.

Home of several generations of distinguished women authors and activists, the Wayside shows their community's many connections and their nation's struggles

At the Wayside, **Louisa May Alcott** began her writing career while living with her artist sister May and reformer mother Abigail. Later, Nathaniel Hawthorne's wife Sophia Peabody

---

DON'T MISS

- Free exhibits in the Wayside Barn
- Nathaniel Hawthorne's "Sky Parlor"
- Road to Revolution at the Minute Man Visitor Center
- The Minute Man statue and the North Bridge

Hawthorne enjoyed being a wife, mother, and artist. Sophia's sister Mary Peabody Mann, widow of educator Horace Mann, lived at the Wayside. Sophia's daughter Rose Hawthorne Lathrop, as Mother Mary Alphonsa, founded the religious order Servants of Relief for Incurable Cancer in 1901. Harriett Lothrop (no relation to the Lathrops) wrote *The Five Little Peppers and How they Grew* under the pen name Margaret Sidney. Her daughter Margaret Lothrop researched and wrote *The Wayside: Home of Authors*; she sold the Wayside to the National Park Service in 1965.

FACILITIES

Minute Man National Historical Park interprets the events of

April 19, 1775, which started the American Revolutionary War and the creation of an American literary identity. Each of three units—the North Bridge, Battle Road, and Wayside—has a visitor center with an Eastern National bookstore. The Wayside witnessed over 300 years of history as home to the Alcotts, the Hawthornes, and the Lothrops, among others.

PROGRAMS

Rangers give talks daily at North Bridge and Hartwell Tavern in season; education programs are available spring and fall. Special programs are featured Patriots' Day through Veterans' Day. The Wayside is open Memorial Day through October.

COLLECTIONS

The Harriett Lothrop Family Papers preserve evidence of the life and work of Harriett Lothrop, historic preservationist and author; her husband Daniel Lothrop; and their daughter, Margaret Lothrop. The papers contain personal correspondence, financial records, handwritten manuscripts, and research materials, including clippings, magazines, photographs, and prints.

Margaret Lothrop (1884-1970) with a visitor to the Wayside. Photograph courtesy of the NPS.

Wayside: Home of Authors. Photograph courtesy of the NPS.

Minute Man
National Historical Park
174 Liberty Street
Concord, MA 01742
978-369-6993
www.nps.gov/mima

Check hours before visiting. North Bridge Unit is open daily. Wayside and Battle Road Units are open seasonally, Memorial Day – Columbus Day. Closed Thanksgiving, Christmas, and New Year's.

Mitchell House, The Nantucket Maria Mitchell Association

NANTUCKET, MASSACHUSETTS

www.mmo.org

Maria Mitchell, c. 1865.

Explore, educate, enjoy!

Maria Mitchell (1818-1889), America's first female astronomer, discovered a telescopic comet in 1847. One of the first women to work for the U.S. federal government, she was hired by the U.S. Nautical Almanac. Mitchell was the first professor hired by Vassar College (1865-1888). She was also a founder of the Association for the Advancement of Women and the first female member of the American Academy of Arts and Sciences. Her birthplace has been the center of the Association since its founding in 1902.

FACILITIES

Visitors take guided tours through the Mitchell House, the home where Maria Mitchell was born and lived with her family until 1836. The House remains in its 19th-century state and holds an exceptional collection of Mitchell family artifacts and papers. Visitors can also take tours of the Maria Mitchell Observatory next door, the natural science museum, the aquarium, and the Loines Observatory for night observations.

DON'T MISS

- The birthplace of Maria Mitchell, a museum since 1902
- The Association's observatories, natural science museum, and aquarium
- Her personal desk and shelves—built into the stair landing

PROGRAMS

The Mitchell House offers guided tours as well as classes for both children and adults, all of which highlight the remarkable contributions of Maria Mitchell and her family to astronomy and education in the 19th century. Nature and bird walks, children's classes, open nights at the observatory, marine walks, and a myriad of other programs year round support Maria Mitchell's and the Association's philosophy of learning by doing.

Mitchell House (built 1790), birthplace of Maria Mitchell, America's first woman astronomer, and Maria Mitchell Observatory (built 1908).

COLLECTIONS

The collections include the papers and manuscripts of Maria Mitchell and family members, artifacts, Maria Mitchell's telescopes, and their personal libraries. The Association also

"We especially need imagination in science. It is not all mathematics, nor all logic, but it is somewhat beauty and poetry."

– Maria Mitchell

maintains a large natural science collection of Nantucket birds and an herbarium; a large glass plate collection of the night sky taken at the observatory since 1916; and, in the summer, a large collection of live organisms native to Nantucket's land and waters.

**The Nantucket
Maria Mitchell Association
4 Vestal Street
Nantucket, MA 02554
508-228-9198
Fax 508-228-1031
info@mmo.org
www.mmo.org**

**Check hours before visiting.
Open Monday through Saturday 10 a.m. -
4 p.m. mid June through Labor Day;
Saturday and Sunday through Columbus
Day. Programming year round.**

Women's History Tours of the Twin Cities

MINNEAPOLIS & ST. PAUL, MINNESOTA

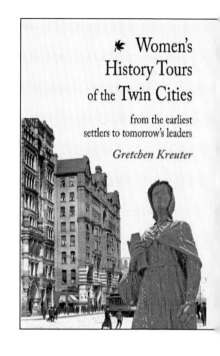

The **Women's History Tours of the Twin Cities** Guide is an invitation to explore the contributions made by women to the history of the cities of Minneapolis and St. Paul.

The tours reach back to the earliest white settlements, exploring historic sites associated with the lives of Jane Gibbs, Harriet Bishop, Clara Ueland, and other pioneers of Twin Cities civic life. The book also describes many recent contributions made by women to their Minnesota communities and institutions.

During the 1970s, '80s, and '90s, new definitions of "women's space" arose, transforming our understanding of women's history and experience. In landmark legal battles over university tenure and workplace discrimination; in women-centered bookstores, cafes and music festivals; and in Pride parades and Take Back the Night marches, local women have commandeered access to a wide variety of spaces previously denied to them.

Today, more than ever, as readers of these tours will find, women's history is everywhere.

Women's History Tours of the Twin Cities

by Gretchen Kreuter

**Available from
Adventure Publications
800-678-7006
Fax 877-374-9016**

Introduction to Resources Section

THE NATIONAL PARK SERVICE, while best known for its parks and historic sites, has long had partnerships with the states and localities. Together, they work to preserve historic places and interpret them to the public. The Travel Itineraries, the Teaching with Historic Places lesson plans, and the Museum Management collections that follow all provide easily accessible information on different kinds of historic and archeological resources. The editor has reviewed these to ferret out women's presence and history in them. Given the tours' architectural emphasis, lack of women identified on a tour should not be assumed to have been the historical situation. Historians need to assume that women were present—and to find them. Because historically most women lived as part of their families, searching for them as wives, daughters, sisters, aunts, etc., greatly increases their ability to be "found" again.

Few people remember women Goldrushers at Klondike Gold Rush in Skagway, Alaska, or park ranger wives at Wupatki's ancient pueblos in Arizona, or architects at the Grand Canyon, or army wives in Yellowstone—but they were all there. More people need to consider the lives of women thousands of years ago, grinding corn on their *metates*, making exquisite pottery, or weaving yucca sandals. A small brass thimble from Jamestown or the carefully divided architecture of the Friends (Quaker) meeting house at Herbert Hoover National Historic Site in Iowa also show us earlier generations of women. Civil War Battlefields that were previously some unlucky families' fields and homes (Gettysburg, Petersburg) need to be seen for the women who once lived there, who endured battles and sieges (Vicksburg), who cared for wounded and dying, who became widows and children of soldiers wounded or killed, and especially African Americans who were now freed from slavery because of that same war. These are so much larger images than simply the military tactics so often presented.

Reading: Women in Books and Articles (Bibliography)

Websurfing: Women in National Park Service Museum Collections (Online Exhibits)

Teaching: Women at Historic Places (Lesson Plans)

Traveling: Women in Tours and Travel Itineraries (Going There!)

Reading: Women in Books and Articles (Bibliography)

Editor's Note: The books listed below are chosen because they are particularly applicable to preserving and interpreting women's history at historic sites. They are also thoughtful additions to our understanding of past women's lives, and they bring different perspectives to our understandings. Many more sources could have been chosen. Books have been chosen over articles because of access issues—sadly, most historic sites lack access to www.jstor.org, rich in academic articles.

REFERENCE WORKS

Hewitt, Nancy A., ed. *A Companion to American Women's History.* Blackwell Companions to American History. New York: Oxford University Press, Oxford 2005.

Hine, Darlene Clark; Elsa Barkley Brown; and Rosalyn Terborg-Penn; eds. *Black Women in America: An Historical Encyclopedia.* Bloomington: Indiana University Press, 1993.

Howe, Barbara J.; Dolores A. Fleming; Emory L. Kemp; and Ruth Ann Overbeck. *Houses and Homes: Exploring their History.* Nashville: American Association for State and Local History, 1987. Thoughtful introduction to sources for analyzing domestic architecture; one in a series. See also Eleanor McD. Thompson, editor, *The American Home: Material Culture, Domestic Space and Family Life.* Winterthur, Del.: Henry Francis du Pont Winterthur Museum, 1998.

James, Edward T.; Janet Wilson James; and Paul Boyer; eds. *Notable American Women, 1607-1950: A Biographical Dictionary.* Cambridge: Harvard University Press, 1974.

Kessler-Harris, Alice; Kathryn Kish Sklar; and Linda K. Kerber. *U.S. History as Women's History: New Feminist Essays.* Chapel Hill: University of North Carolina Press, 1995.

Ruiz, Vicki L. *From Out of the Shadows: Mexican Women in Twentieth-Century America.* New York: Oxford University Press, 1998.

Sicherman, Barbara; Carol Hurd Green; *et al.,* eds. *Notable American Women: The Modern Period,* [vol. 4]. Cambridge: Harvard, 1980.

Ware, Susan, and Stacey Braukman, eds. *Notable American Women: A Biographical Dictionary, 5, Completing the Twentieth Century.* Cambridge: Harvard University Press, 2004.

READINGS–GENERAL

Bartlett, Virginia K. *Keeping House: Women's Lives in Western Pennsylvania, 1790-1850.* Pittsburgh: University of Pittsburg Press, 1994. With the Historical Society of Western Pennsylvania. Tangible history of a time and area.

Brooks, James F. *Captives & Cousins: Slavery, Kinship, and Community in the Southwest Borderlands.* Chapel Hill: University of North Carolina Press, 2002. Females taken captive in an "exchange network of human beings" of tribal peoples, Hispanics and Anglos–reshaped those groups as cross cultural kinspeople. (Women were 2/3 of all captives.)

Brown, Kathleen M. *Good Wives, Nasty Wenches & Anxious Patriarchs: Gender, Race and Power in Colonial Virginia.* Chapel Hill: University of North Carolina Press, 1996. Greater complexities than schoolbooks guessed.

Campbell, Edward, and Kym S. Rice, eds. *A Woman's War: Southern Women, Civil War, and the Confederate Legacy.* Charlottesville: University Press of Virginia, 1996. Essays on women during the war including refugees and contrabands (African American self-freeing slaves) using accounts, historical photographs, and artifacts from the Civil War era.

Carson, Cary, ed. *Becoming Americans: Our Struggle to Be Both Free and Equal: A Plan of Thematic Interpretation.* Williamsburg, Va.: The Colonial Williamsburg Foundation, 1998. Colonial Williamsburg key themes documented with images, maps, and objects reveal colonial and Revolutionary lives. Written for visitors; good bibliographies.

Clinton, Catherine, ed. *Southern Families at War: Loyalty and Conflict in the Civil War South.* New York: Oxford University Press, 2000.

Domosh, Mona, and Joni Seager. *Putting Women in Place: Feminist Geographers Make Sense of the World.* New York: Guilford Press, 2001. Geographers' perspectives.

Evans, Sara. *Born for Liberty.* New York: Touchstone Books, 1994. Good synthesis.

Faust, Drew Gilpin. *Mothers of Invention: Women of the Slaveholding South in the American Civil War.* New York: Vintage Press, 1996. A different perspective on the Civil War.

Fett, Sharla M. *Working Cures: Healing, Health, and Power on Southern Slave Plantations.* Chapel Hill: University of North Carolina Press, 2002. Enslaved people using their own medical knowledge and practices.

Giddings, Paula. *When and Where I Enter: The Impact of Black Women on Race and Sex in America.* New York: HarperCollins, 1984. African American women have "converted the rock of double oppression into a stepping stone."

Hale, Grace Elizabeth. *Making Whiteness: The Culture of Segregation in the South, 1890-1940*. New York: Vintage Books, 1998. History of Jim Crow, segregation, lynching, consumption, and memory dividing the races and defining blacks and whites. Insightful and gender-full.

Hewitt, Nancy A., and Suzanne Lebsock, eds. *Visible Women: New Essays on American Activism*. Urbana: University of Illinois Press, 1993. Political activism of many kinds, 1870-1940 providing context for sites.

Hine, Darlene Clark, and Kathleen Thompson. *A Shining Thread of Hope: The History of Black Women in America*. New York: Broadway Books, 1998.

Hine, Darlene Clark. *Hinesight: Black Women and the Re-Construction of American History*. Brooklyn, N.Y.: Carlson Publication, 1994. See especially "Rape and the Inner Lives of Black Women: Thoughts on the Culture of Dissemblance."

Hunter, Tera W. *To 'Joy My Freedom: Southern Black Women's Lives and Labors after the Civil War*. Cambridge: Harvard University Press, 1997.

Klepp, Susan E. "Lost, Hidden, Obstructed, and Repressed: Contraceptive and Abortive Technology in the Early Delaware Valley." In *Early American Technology: Making & Doing Things from the Colonial Era to 1850*, edited by Judith A. McGaw. Chapel Hill: University of North Carolina Press, 1994. Family planning history.

Irwin, Mary Ann, and James F. Brooks, eds. *Women and Gender in the American West: Jensen-Miller Prize Essays from the Coalition for Western Women's History*. Albuquerque: University of New Mexico Press, 2004. From British Columbia to New Mexico, 15th to 20th century, different women's lives.

Jensen, Joan M. *Loosening the Bonds: Mid-Atlantic Farm Women, 1750-1850*. New Haven: Yale University Press, 1986. Women's economic centrality to their agricultural families in the Philadelphia butter belt.

Joyner, Brian D. *African Reflections on the American Landscape*. Washington, D.C.: National Park Service, 2003. Excellent.

Joyner, Brian D. *Asian Reflections on the American Landscape: Identifying and Interpreting Asian Heritage*. Washington, D.C.: National Park Service, 2005.

Norling, Lisa. *Captain Ahab Had a Wife: New England Women and Whalefishery, 1720-1870*. Chapel Hill: University of North Carolina Press, 2000. Lives of "Cape Horn widows" left behind. (Some 19th-century merchant marine captains' wives traveled with their husbands; see San Francisco Maritime National Historic Site.)

Plane, Ann Marie. *Colonial Intimacies: Indian Marriage in Early New England*. Ithaca: Cornell University Press, 2000.

Ruiz, Vicki, and Ellen Carol DuBois, eds. *Unequal Sisters: A Multicultural Reader in U.S. Women's History.* 4th ed. New York: Routledge, 2007. Excellent collection of articles.

Spain, Daphne. *How Women Saved the City.* Minneapolis: University of Minnesota Press, 2001. Voluntary organizations and "redemptive places" women formed to meet urban needs.

READINGS–HISTORIC SITES, PRESERVATION, AND INTERPRETATION

Ames, Kenneth L. *Death in the Dining Room & Other Tales of Victorian Culture.* Philadelphia: Temple University Press, 1992. Victorian material culture gives insights into domesticity and women's lives.

Casper, Scott E. *Sarah Johnson's Mount Vernon: The Forgotten History of an American Shrine.* New York: Hill and Wang, 2008. Mount Vernon from the perspective of African Americans who lived there in slavery and freedom, focusing on Sarah Johnson. A counterpoint to the Mount Vernon Ladies Association.

Dubrow, Gail Lee, and Jennifer B. Goodman, eds. *Restoring Women's History through Historic Preservation.* Baltimore: Johns Hopkins Press, 2003. Essays.

Hayden, Dolores. *The Power of Place: Urban Landscapes as Public History.* Cambridge: MIT Press, 1995. Exploring different lives, places, and meanings from 19th-century Los Angeles' black midwife Biddy Mason to Little Tokyo and Public Memory.

Huyck, Heather. "Beyond John Wayne: Using Historic Sites to Interpret Women's History." In *Western Women: Their Land, Their Lives,* edited by Lillian Schlissel, Vicki L. Ruiz, and Janice Monk. Albuquerque: University of New Mexico Press, 1988.

Huyck, Heather, ed. National Park Service's *CRM* issue: "Placing Women in the Past," 20:3 (1997). Special issue specifically dealing with women at various National Park Service sites. Available online at http://crm.cr.nps.gov/archive/20-3/20-3-2.pdf

Kaufman, Polly Welts, and Katharine T. Corbett, eds. *Her Past around Us: Interpreting Sites for Women's History.* Malabar, Fla.: Krieger Publishing, 2003.

Levy, Barbara Abramoff. *Great Tours: Thematic Tours and Guide Training for Historic Sites.* Walnut Creek, Cal.: AltaMira Press, 2001.

Lower East Side Tenement Museum. *A Tenement Story: The History of 97 Orchard Street and the Lower East Side Tenement Museum.* New York: Lower East Side Tenement Museum, 2004.

Miller, Page Putnam. "Landmarks of Women's History." In *Reclaiming the Past: Landmarks of Women's History,* edited by Page Putnam Miller. Bloomington: Indiana University Press, 1992.

Miller, Page Putnam. *Landmarks of American Women's History.* New York: Oxford University Press, 2004.

National Park Service. *Exploring a Common Past: Interpreting Women's History in the National Park Service.* Washington, D.C.: National Park Service, 2005. Sections by Anne Derousie, Sara Evans, Shaun Eyring and Leslie Sharp. Available on line at http://www.nps.gov/history/history/hisnps/npshistory/womenshistory.pdfany

National Park Service. Handbooks. Various dates. Guides to specific NPS sites; well illustrated and useful.

Savage, Beth L., ed. *African American Historic Places: National Register of Historic Places.* Washington, D.C.: Preservation Press, 1994. Several historic essays and extensive lists of sites preserving African American history. Key Guide.

Sherr, Lynn, and Jurate Kazickas. *Susan B. Anthony Slept Here: A Guide to American Women's Landmarks.* New York: Times Books, 1994. Popular treatment.

Tinling, Marion. *Women Remembered: A Guide to Landmarks of Women's History in the United States.* New York: Greenwood Press, 1986.

READINGS–MATERIAL CULTURE/TANGIBLE RESOURCES

Adams, Annmarie, and Sally McMurry, eds. *Exploring Everyday Landscapes: Perspectives in Vernacular Architecture.* Knoxville: University of Tennessee Press, 1997. Vernacular Architecture Forum books often have chapters on women's creation and use of architecture, landscapes, and space in general. High quality.

Campbell, Edward, and Kym S. Rice, eds. *Before Freedom Came: African-American Life in the Antebellum South.* Charlottesville: University Press of Virginia, 1991. Images, photographs, maps, and objects—some beautiful, others horrific—documenting various experiences of slavery. Considerable attention to women. Excellent.

Cooney, Robert P. J., Jr. *Winning the Vote: The Triumph of the American Woman Suffrage Movement.* Santa Cruz, Cal.: American Graphic Press, 2005. Terrific images.

Cowan, Ruth Schwartz. "Coal Stoves and Clean Sinks: Housework between 1890 and 1930." In *American Home Life, 1880-1930: A Social History of Spaces and Services*, edited by Jessica H. Foy and Thomas J. Schlereth. Knoxville: University of Tennessee Press, 1992.

Dolkart, Andrew S. *Biography of a Tenement House in New York City: An Architectural History of 97 Orchard Street.* Santa Fe, N.M.: The Center for American Places, Inc., 2007. History of a tenement 1864-1935, its immigrant residents' lives, as embodied in a specific building now preserved and open to the public. Door to another world.

Floyd, Tom. *Lost Trails and Forgotten People: The Story of Jones Mountain.* Washington, D.C.: Potomac Appalachian Trail Club, 1981. Using historic photographs and physical remnants (stone walls and chimneys) to tell story of families who lived in Virginia's mountain before it became Shenandoah National Park—"national parks" have *cultural* resources.

Foy, Jessica H., and Thomas J. Schlereth, eds. *American Home Life, 1880-1930: A Social History of Spaces and Services.* Knoxville: University of Tennessee Press, 1992.

Herman, Bernard. L. "The Embedded Landscapes of the Charleston Single House, 1780-1820." In *Exploring Everyday Landscapes: Perspectives in Vernacular Architecture, VII,* edited by Annmarie Adams and Sally McMurry. Knoxville: University of Tennessee Press, 1997.

Hunter, Christine. *Ranches, Rowhouses and Railroad Flats: American Homes: How They Shape Our Landscapes and Neighborhoods.* New York: W. W. Norton & Company, Inc., 1999. Domestic space analyzed to understand 19th- and 20th-century changing American lives.

Johnson, Walter. *Soul by Soul: Life Inside the Antebellum Slave Market.* Cambridge, Mass.: Harvard University Press, 1999. Slavery, slaves, and physical evidence.

Little, Barbara J. *Historical Archaeology: Why the Past Matters.* Walnut Creek, Cal.: Left Coast Press, Inc., 2007. Varied examples of research and interpretation, from 17th-century Jamestown to a 16th-century Florida mission to a 18th-century African burial ground and a 19th-century Jewish Five Points tenement in NYC.

Martin, Ann Smart. "Material Things and Cultural Meanings: Notes on the Study of Early American Material Culture." *William and Mary Quarterly* 53:1 (January 1996).

Martinez, Katharine, and Kenneth L. Ames, eds. *The Material Culture of Gender, the Gender of Material Culture.* Winterthur, Del.: Henry Francis du Pont Winterthur Museum, 1997.

McMurry, Sally. *Families & Farmhouses in Nineteenth Century America: Vernacular Design and Social Change.* Knoxville: University of Tennessee Press, 1997. Women's kitchens showing their improved status.

Roth, Rodris. "Tea-Drinking in Eighteenth Century America: Its Etiquette and Equipage." In *Material Life in America, 1600-1800,* edited by Robert Blair St. George. Boston: Northeastern University Press, 1988.

Sagstetter, Bill, and Beth Sagstetter. *The Mining Camps Speak: A New Way to Explore the Ghost Towns of the American West.* Denver: Benchmark Publishing of Colorado, 1998. Women living in overwhelmingly male 19th-century worlds as wives, daughters, teachers, nurses, or prostitutes and by taking in laundry or boarders.

St. George, Robert Blair. "Witchcraft, Bodily Affliction, and Domestic Space in Seventeenth-Century New England." In *A Centre of Wonders: The Body in Early America,* edited by Janet Moore Lindman and Michele Lise Tarter. Ithaca, N.Y.: Cornell University Press, 2001.

Sanfilippo, Pamela. "Sunshine and Shadow: Free Space/Slave Space at White Haven." In *Her Past around Us: Interpreting Sites for Women's History*, edited by Polly Welts Kaufman and Katharine T. Corbett. Malabar, Fla.: Krieger Publishing, 2003.

Schlereth, Thomas J. "Mail-Order Catalogs as Resources in Material Culture Studies." In *Cultural History and Material Culture: Everyday Life, Landscapes, Museums*. Charlottesville: University Press of Virginia, 1992.

Sewell, Jessica. "Gender, Imagination, and Experience in the Early-Twentieth-Century American Downtown." In *Everyday America: Cultural Landscape Studies after J. B. Jackson*, edited by Chris Wilson and Paul Groth. Berkeley: University of California Press, 2003.

Smith, Bonnie Hurd. "Women's Voices: Reinterpreting Historic House Museums." *Her Past around Us: Interpreting Sites for Women's History*, edited by Polly Welts Kaufman and Katharine T. Corbett. Malabar, Fla.: Krieger Publishing, 2003.

Spain, Daphne. *Gendered Spaces*. Chapel Hill: University of North Carolina Press, 1992. An intellectual framework for the *places/spaces* of historic sites.

Thompson, Eleanor, ed. *The American Home: Material Culture, Domestic Space and Family Life*. Winterthur, Del.: University Press of New England, 1998.

Travis, Tara. "Spider Women's Grand Design: Making Native American Women Visible in Two Southwestern History Sites." In *Her Past around Us: Interpreting Sites for Women's History*, edited by Polly Welts Kaufman and Katharine T. Corbett. Malabar, Fla: Krieger Publishing, 2003.

Ulrich, Laurel Thatcher. *Age of Homespun: Objects and Stories in the Creation of an American Myth*. New York: Random House, 2001. Mind-opening essays.

Vlach, John Michael. *Back of the Big House: An Architecture of Plantation Slavery*. Chapel Hill: University of North Carolina Press, 1993. Classic analysis of 18th- to 19th-century housing on plantations where most blacks lived—as enslaved people. Extensive photographs.

Weiner, Lynn. "Women and Work" in *Reclaiming the Past: Landmarks of Women's History*, edited by Page Putnam Miller. Bloomington: Indiana University Press, 1992.

Websurfing: Women in National Park Service Museum Collections (Online Exhibits)

First Ladies Martha Washington, Mamie Eisenhower, Bess Truman, Mary Todd Lincoln, Eleanor Roosevelt; rancher Augusta Kohrs; American Red Cross founder Clara Barton; banker Maggie Walker; Arlington's lady of the house Mary Custis Lee and its enslaved housekeeper Selina Grey; Pueblo potter Maria Martinez; champion goat breeder Lillian Steichen Sandburg; and suffragist Elizabeth Cady Stanton. . . . These are some of the many women represented in National Park Service's more than 120 million item museum collections located at over 360 park sites nationwide. Collections–cared for in the very places where they were made or used–include objects, historic photographs, and documents. Tangible, they have immediacy, authenticity, and give unique historical perspectives. The collections connect visitors directly to, and give insights into, women's personal and public lives, family, home, interests, and social life.

National Park Service virtual museum exhibits and online *Teaching with Museum Collections* lesson plans (at www.nps.gov/history/museum) allow visitors to examine closely Pablita Velarde's artwork, Maria Martinez' pottery, 1950s fashion icon Mamie Eisenhower's often pink wardrobe, Mary Todd Lincoln's home furnishings (and white cake recipe), Eleanor Roosevelt's Val-Kill home, and Bess Truman's family portraits (and meatloaf recipe). Collection-based lesson plans accompany the virtual exhibits. Exhibits include:

Arlington House: The Robert E. Lee Memorial, Arlington, Virginia. Here lived Mary Custis Lee, great-granddaughter of Martha Washington and her daughters; enslaved housekeeper Selina Grey and many other women, free and slave; and buried here, Mary Randolph, author of the first truly American cookbook, *The Virginia Housewife.*

Bandelier National Monument, Bandelier, New Mexico. Works Project Administration Santa Clara artist Pablita Velarde worked here, and San Ildefonso Pueblo potter Maria Martinez lived and worked nearby.

Cowboys to Cattlemen: Augusta Kohrs at Grant-Kohrs Ranch NHS, Deer Lodge, Montana. Mrs. Augusta Kohrs lived on these high plains during the transition to huge cattle ranching operations. She visited Venice, Italy, as well.

Frederick Douglass: American Visionary. Douglass, long a supporter of women's rights, married Anna Murray Douglass (1813-1882) and, after her death, Helen Pitts Douglass (1838-1903). He knew Susan B. Anthony, Elizabeth Cady Stanton, and Harriet Tubman. The National Association of Colored Women saved his Washington, D.C., home, Cedar Hill.

Dwight D. Eisenhower and Mamie Eisenhower at their Gettysburg farm in Pennsylvania. Mrs. Eisenhower (1896-1979) loved the color pink—wearing it and painting their home with it. She stated, "I have but one career, and his name is Ike."

Eleanor Roosevelt (1884-1962) met friends, family, and international visitors at her beloved Val-Kill home in Hyde Park, New York. Her personal possessions included a fancy tape dispenser, silver nut dishes, and Val-Kill industries reproduction colonial furniture. She traveled worldwide as her president husband FDR's eyes and ears; after his death she focused on humanitarian and political causes.

Guilford National Military Park: Women of the American Revolutionary War. Women kept the family farms going and experienced war firsthand.

Abraham Lincoln and Mary Todd Lincoln (1818-1882). Mary Todd Lincoln's rocking chair in Springfield, Illinois, at the only home they owned. She loved to entertain and be fashionable but also spent considerable time sewing clothes for her sons and husband.

Harry S. Truman and Bess Truman (1895-1982). Bess Truman at home in Independence, Missouri. Her wedding anniversary plate, telegrams with Queen Elizabeth II concerning her mother's death, and her dog Jip provide insights to this first lady.

Carl Sandburg and Lillian Steichen Sandburg (1883-1977) at Connemara, North Carolina. He was famous for his literary prizes; she, for her prize-winning dairy goat herds. With her careful goat breeding and records, she became "a legend in the dairy goat industry." See www.nps.gov/carl.

For further information, please contact the National Park Service, Park Museum Management Program, 1201 Eye Street, NW, Washington, DC 20005. Special thanks to Ms. Joan Bacharach for her contributions to this work.

Teaching: Women at Historic Places (Lesson Plans)

Teaching with Historic Places has developed more than 130 classroom-ready lesson plans that together range across American history. All are available in their entirety on the web at the National Park Service site: http://www.nps.gov/history/NR/twhp.

The descriptions below have been excerpted from that site, with an emphasis on women's history. For more information, see the original lessons and, sometimes, their National Historic Landmark nomination and/or National Park Service website for National Historic Sites and other units of the National Park System at www.nps.gov.

The number after each lesson title refers to its NPS identification number. National Historic Landmarks have been so designated by the Secretary of the Interior. Places now part of national park system have their website listed beginning with www.nps.gov/.

Lessons That Feature Women

Memories of Montpelier: Home of James and Dolley Madison (46)

Dolley Payne Madison (1768-1849) lost her first husband, John Todd, and their son to the 1793 yellow fever epidemic in Philadelphia. She married James Madison in 1794, a long and happy marriage. During his public life, Madison's service included the first Continental Congress, the Virginia Assembly (for five years), the Federal Convention, U.S. Congress, secretary of state, and, finally, president, 1809-1817. She became the first lady. A noted hostess and lively person, she escaped the British burning of the young nation's capital city in 1814, fleeing with George Washington's portrait. In 1817, the Madisons retired home to his 5,000-acre family estate in the Virginia piedmont, where they became widely known for their gracious hospitality. The more than 100 enslaved African Americans who worked and lived at Montpelier helped support their lifestyle. National Historic Landmark.

From Canterbury to Little Rock: The Struggle for Educational Equality for African Americans

Canterbury

In 1831, Canterbury, Connecticut, parents asked 27-year-old Quaker Prudence Crandall (1803-1890) to open a private school to teach their

101

young women. She responded by opening the Canterbury Female Boarding School. With strong community support, the school succeeded. The next year, an African American girl, Sarah Harris, asked Prudence Crandall to let her attend the school; Crandall, a staunch abolitionist, agreed. But the Canterbury community objected strongly, threatening to withdraw their daughters if Harris remained in the school. Crandall, who believed that African American girls also deserved an education, then reopened the school the following year specifically to educate "young ladies and little misses of color." Town leaders tried to convince her to abandon her efforts to teach black girls. Crandall recruited three girls, eventually teaching 24 students. Teacher and students faced harassment and an attempt to burn down the school. In response, the Connecticut General Assembly enacted the "Black Law" against black education. Crandall violated it and spent a night in jail; her case was later dismissed on a technicality. Then, in 1834, a mob broke into the school and ransacked it, terrorizing the students and breaking more than 90 windows. What the Black Law and local ostracism had not accomplished, the mob achieved. Fearing for her black female students' safety, Crandall closed the school the next morning. National Historic Landmark.

Little Rock

In 1954, the U.S. Supreme Court ruled in *Brown v. Board of Education* that "separate but equal" accommodations in education were not constitutional. Later they decreed that desegregation was to occur with "all deliberate speed." Little Rock schools planned for the 1957 desegregation, beginning with the high school, with Little Rock Central High School to begin in September 1957. That summer opposition grew from a white citizens' council. Legal actions and counter actions followed. Emotions rose and Little Rock gained national attention. On September 24, President Eisenhower surprised the nation by federalizing the National Guard to ensure the desegregation effort and to protect the African American students. Nine students enrolled. One girl, Melba Pattillo Beals, remembered later, "My eight friends and I paid for the integration of Central High with our innocence. During those years when we desperately needed approval from our peers, we were victims of the most harsh rejection imaginable. The physical and psychological punishment we endured profoundly affected our lives. It transformed us into warriors who dared not cry even when we suffered intolerable pain." See Melba Pattillo Beals, *Warriors Don't Cry: A Searing Memoir of the Battle to Integrate Little Rock's Central High* (New York: Washington Square Press, 1994), p. 2. See also www.nps.gov/liro.

The M'Clintock House: A Home to the Women's Rights Movement (76)

Liberal Quakers who believed in the equality of men and women, the M'Clintocks lived near Seneca Falls in upstate New York. They hosted a small group of women for tea. Together the women planned the 1848 Women's Rights Convention and wrote its "Declaration of Sentiments" (based on the Declaration of Independence), which called for major changes in the status and opportunities of American women. Nine days later, 200 people gathered at the Seneca Falls Wesleyan Chapel, debated the issues, and adopted that Declaration. It covered everything from women's education, family and marriage rights, and professional opportunities to religious attitudes. They also called for women to be formally recognized politically by getting the vote (suffrage). In 1920, enough states ratified the U.S. Constitution that women finally got the vote. For more information, see also www.nps.gov/wori.

The Battle of Prairie Grove: Civilian Recollections of the Civil War (70)

This 1862 Arkansas Civil War battle, as seen by young women whose homes became the battlefield, with their families hiding in basements; with wounded, dying, and dead soldiers all around their homes; sometimes, their own homes burned down; and with looters demanding their money–a mixture of terror and horror.

Clara Barton's House: Home of the American Red Cross (27)

She taught school, worked as the only female clerk in the U.S. government's patent office, volunteered as a nurse on Civil War battlefields, founded the American Red Cross in 1881, and created "First Aid." Clara Barton (1821-1912) spent four years identifying more than 22,000 missing Civil War soldiers. A proponent of women's rights, she spoke at the First International Woman's Suffrage Conference in Washington, D.C. In 1891, she constructed a 10,000-square-foot building just outside Glen Echo, Maryland, to serve as her home and the headquarters of her fledgling organization. Here she stored relief supplies, housed staff, and lived herself. Gifts from various grateful individuals and organizations decorated it. The first floor also had her offices, with American Red Cross stained glass windows in their doors and early typewriters, graphophones, and telephone–evidence of their activity and seriousness of purpose. This lesson plan provides her biographical information. For more information on the house, see also www.nps.gov/clba. Nationally and internationally recognized, she died in 1912 at age 90, having lived a long life changing many peoples' lives. She received medals and decorations from Germany, Turkey, Serbia, and the International Red Cross. See also www.nps.gov/clba and *Clara Barton National Park Service Handbook 110*, 1981.

Adeline Hornbek and the Homestead Act: A Colorado Success Story (67)

A single mother of four children, Hornbek defied traditional gender expectations and, using the 1862 Homestead Act, for 27 years ranched successfully—in the Rocky Mountains at 10,000 feet above sea level. Her homestead remains, including her two-story, four-bedroom log house with a milk house, chicken house, and stables as its outbuildings. Widowed once, and abandoned by another husband, she chose her ranch location well—with an abundant water supply, fertile soil, large meadows for grazing cattle, and Ponderosa pine forests. She also worked in the nearby general store to earn the cash she needed. Nearby transportation allowed her to ship her cattle to market. Hornbek became a prominent member of the Florissant community, serving on its school board and hosting social gatherings in her Victorian home. She died in 1905. (Other women also used the Homestead Act to gain land for themselves. A famous Nebraska Solomon Butcher photograph shows the four Chrisman sisters on their homestead claims. Successfully "proving up" a claim entailed lots of very hard work, resources, and luck.) See also www.nps.gov/flfo.

Two American Entrepreneurs: Madam C. J. Walker and J. C. Penney

Madam C. J. Walker

Walker made her late 19th-century to early 20th-century fortune selling hair and beauty products to African American women. The Walker Building in Indianapolis, Indiana, with its African details, served as the headquarters for the Madam C. J. Walker Manufacturing Company, a business that once employed 3,000 African American women and men to manufacture and to sell hair products and cosmetics for African American women as trained door-to-door salespeople ("Walker Agents"). She envisioned that the building (completed after her 1919 death at age 52) would be a social and cultural center for African Americans in Indianapolis. Walker (no relation to Maggie Walker of Richmond, Virginia) had invented hair care and beauty products specifically for black women in the decades following their emancipation from slavery. Born in 1867 Louisiana, she had also been a cook and washerwoman but wanted to be an entrepreneur. She stated, "I have made it possible for many colored women to abandon the wash-tub for more pleasant and profitable occupation[s]." She became very wealthy, an enormous accomplishment for an African American woman during Jim Crow.

Walker enjoined black women: "Don't sit down and wait for the opportunities to come. Get up and make them!" Walker also supported various black causes, serving on the National Association for the Advancement of Colored People (NAACP) national board. In 1912, left off the agenda of Booker T. Washington's National Negro Business League, she took over the podium, successfully demanding to be heard. After she died, many people mourned her accomplishments and her generosity. Her daughter A'Lelia carried on her mission. Madam C. J. Walker had once proclaimed, "Perseverance is my motto!" Page Putnam Miller, "Madam C. J. Walker Building" (Marion County, Indiana) National Historic Landmark Nomination Form, Washington, D.C.: U.S. Department of the Interior, National Park Service, 1990; and A'Lelia Perry Bundles, *Madam C. J. Walker: Entrepreneur* (New York: Chelsea House Publishers, 1991). National Historic Landmark.

J. C. Penney

When he first opened a store in Kemmerer, Wyoming, in 1902, James Cash Penney wanted to provide quality dry goods at reasonable prices to a growing middle class, especially in the West. His Golden Rule Stores sold men's, women's, and children's clothing; shoes; notions; and fabric for sewing. It became the first national department store chain. By 1921, he had opened 313 stores in Utah, Idaho, Nevada, Oregon, Washington, and Colorado; ten years later (during the Great Depression) there were 1,250 J. C. Penney stores. The company sold merchandise for cash only (no credit) in small towns stores without fancy displays and worked hard to give good value. The "Penney Idea" included treating all customers well and "reward[ing] men and women in our organization through participation in what the business produces." When he died in 1971 his stores had successfully spread nationwide and moved into suburbia. The company continues today. These stores sold *ready-made clothes*—rather than having mothers sewing their family's clothes or hiring seamstresses to make them. Many women moved towards being consumers rather than producers of goods. National Historic Landmark.

Back Stairs at Brucemore: Life as Servants in Early 20th-Century America (105)

In 1906, the Douglass family moved to their new estate in Cedar Rapids, Iowa, their wealth coming from a large corn processing factory. The large home had a swimming pool, tennis courts, greenhouse, and extensive formal gardens. The family's leisure activities and civic contributions contrasted with the servant workforce that made their lifestyle possible. By the early 20th century, servants were often immigrants or African Americans, working as a butler, chauffeur/car mechanic, maid, housekeeper, nanny, and gardener. These jobs contrasted with factory work that gave greater personal privacy but more structured work. Working-class women by necessity had "freedom" to work (in other peoples' homes) while upper-class women were expected to remain in their homes. National Register of Historic Places.

The Mary McLeod Bethune Council House: African American Women Unite for Change (135)

Mary McLeod Bethune (1875-1955) founded the National Council of Negro Women in 1935, bringing black women together to fight for integration of blacks into schools and the military and to fight against discrimination in housing, healthcare, and employment. Bethune, founder of Bethune-Cookman College in Florida and a key advisor on blacks to the administration of President Franklin Delano Roosevelt, worked hard to improve their too often abysmal situations. See also www.nps.gov/mamc.

Floyd Bennett Field (120)

Originally a civilian airfield, this became a naval airbase during World War II for naval patrol squadrons. Floyd Bennett Field had the mission to "to provide base facilities for the Fleet and the North Atlantic Naval Frontier, and to assemble, service, equip, and deliver naval aircraft from factory to fleet." NAS Beam: *U.S. Naval Air Station New York Floyd Bennett Field* (Baton Rouge, La.: Army and Navy Publishing Co., 1944).

After the December 1941 Japanese attack on Pearl Harbor in December 1941, the field's mission quickly expanded to include patrolling for submarines, scouting for the enemy, and transporting airplanes. Women played key roles at the airbase during the war. Navy WAVES (Women Accepted for Volunteer Exceptional Service) operated radio equipment out of the control tower, directing traffic at this busiest naval air station in the nation, while others packed parachutes for use by aviators or served as aviation machinist mates ("plane captains"). One WAVE, Josephine (Camerlengo) Tanner, later remembered that she was "responsible for having every aircraft properly assembled and kept in satisfactory flying condition, as well as overhauling engines on a regular basis. . . . I was plane captain to a crew of three men. My signature was on the paper that released the serviced aircraft for ferrying to the West Coast." See Fran Boggs Metcalf, Amy May Foster Feluk, and Josephine Camerlengo Tanner, *"Memories of the Service Careers of Three Navy W.A.V.E.S."* 22 March 2004, Floyd Bennett Field Task Force Collection, Brooklyn, New York. Now part of Jamaica Bay Unit of Gateway National Recreation Area, See also www.nps.gov/gate.

First Lady of the World: Eleanor Roosevelt at Val-Kill (26)

Her husband Franklin Delano Roosevelt joked about his wife Eleanor Roosevelt (1884-1962) wanting a country retreat, a less formal place than the nearby Hyde Park mansion they shared with his mother Sara Delano Roosevelt. Eleanor Roosevelt initially used the stone cottage Val-Kill and later opened a furniture factory, built two miles away, to be with her friends. These women included her special friend reporter Lorena Hickok. After FDR's 1945 death, she moved there. She had declared "the story is over," then but her very full if complex life still had several key chapters before her 1962 death. She had traveled for her disabled husband during the Great Depression and World War II; now she traveled arguing for the United Nation's Declaration of Human Rights— a document still timely in its statements, if still unfulfilled in its demands. Val-Kill shows her personal life and political life. Here she said, "I emerged as an individual." See also www.nps.gov/elro.

Lesson Plans That Include But Do Not Focus on Women

Pre-contact

Gran Quivira: A Blending of Cultures in a Pueblo Indian Village (66)

A thousand years of change in this village from the 7th century to the 17th-century Spanish arrival.

Tonto National Monument: Saving a National Treasure (125)

Salado culture prior to European contact in a harsh and arid environment in Arizona.

Colonial/Revolutionary

Forts of Old San Juan: Guardians of the Caribbean (60)

Spanish forts on the island of Puerto Rico helped protect Spain's expanding Western interests. See also www.nps.gov/saju.

San Antonio Missions: Spanish Influence in Texas (2)

Six missions with churches, *conventos*, walls, and *acequias* (irrigation ditches), these communities combined Franciscan church missions with Spanish military outposts. American Indians (*Coahuiltecans*) and Spanish came together here. Although the Spanish Catholic priests were all males, some of the Spanish soldiers had families living with them and the native peoples living at these 18th-century missions very much included women and girls. See also www.nps.gov/saan.

Saugus Iron Works: Life and Work at an Early American Industrial Site (30)

A mid-17th-century ironworks and village of early European settlers now in Massachusetts where archeological excavations have found spoons, a pewter baby nipple, and other evidence of the workers' wives and families living with them. These Puritans worked hard to create lives for themselves. See also www.nps.gov/sair.

The Vieux Carré: A Creole Neighborhood in New Orleans (20)

New Orleans's distinctive Creole heritage mixed French, Spanish, English, and African peoples together. Founded in 1734, French Ursuline nuns established a charity hospital, orphanage, and school for girls. From 1881 to 1964, Sisters of the Holy Family, a Roman Catholic African American teaching order, had their motherhouse here. See also www.nps.gov/jela.

Bethlehem, Pennsylvania: A Moravian Settlement in Colonial America (59)

German Pietists, the Moravians immigrated in 1741 and built towns that reflected their beliefs and missionary efforts, using the "choir system" that divided members by age and gender into smaller groups. National Register of Historic Places.

Frederica: An 18th-Century Planned Community (31)

A British settlement built to control Spanish expansion into lands from Charleston, South Carolina, to St. Augustine, Florida. The first colonists, selected by Governor James Oglethorpe to ensure Frederica's growth and prosperity, included 44 men and 72 women and children. Initially a military outpost and town established in 1736, this beginning of the colony of Georgia was later researched and promoted as a park by Margaret Davis Cate (1888-1961). See also www.nps.gov/fofr.

Waterford, Virginia: From Mill Town to National Historic Landmark (88)

An 18th-century Quaker farming village, whose mill ground locally grown wheat into flour and whose residents worshiped in their Quaker

(Friends) meeting. Waterford grew into a thriving village that supplied surrounding farms with merchandise, schools, taverns, and the all-important water-run mills. National Historic Landmark.

Independence Hall: International Symbol of Freedom (132)

In spite of Abigail Adams's plea to her husband to "remember the ladies," women were largely ignored in the political documents that founded this nation. Later generations have used those documents to argue for greater female participation and recognition in this nation. Independence Hall stands among colonial port of Philadelphia with lower-class, "middlin," and high-style families there, from slaves and servants to aristocracy. See also www.nps.gov/inde.

Knife River: Early Village Life on the Plains (1)

Taken from her Lemhi Shoshoni tribe as a child, in 1804-1805 Sacagawea (1788-1812) was living at the matrilineal Hidatsa-Mandan's Knife River Indian Villages with her husband Toussaint Charbonneau when they joined the Lewis and Clark expedition. Traveling with her baby Jean-Baptiste, she served as interpreter and guide on the arduous expedition. Her presence told the native peoples they encountered that the American Corps of Discovery came peacefully. See www.nps.gov/knri.

Life on an Island: Early Settlers Off the Rock-Bound Coast of Maine (16)

About 1806, William Gilley and Hannah Lurvey Gilley moved their family from Mount Desert Island to Baker Island, now part of Acadia National Park. During the next decades, the Gilley family fished and farmed and raised a large family with twelve children there, Atlantic coast "pioneers." Hannah Gilley homeschooled their children and in the summertime rowed them across to the mainland for church. See also www.nps.gov/acad.

When Rice Was King (3)

European Americans and enslaved Africans together cultivated rice and grew the plantation world. From the 1730s to the late 19th century, South Carolina grew more rice than any other state. Its cultivation gave rise to a plantation system that depended on slaves brought from Africa to run its complex irrigation systems and provide expert labor forces for the backbreaking work. By the 1740s, 90% of South Carolina's population was black slaves. For nearly a century, this area was the second largest rice producer in the world. Historian Judith A. Carney emphasizes the work that the enslaved women did to cultivate the rice. This lesson plan shows the geography of a slave plantation. See Judith A. Carney, *Black Rice: The African Origins of Rice Cultivation in the Americas* (Cambridge: Harvard University Press, 2002). National Register of Historic Places.

The Battle of Horseshoe Bend: Collision of Cultures (54)

In 1814, European Americans and Creek American Indians fought over their lands and their differences. One thousand warriors and 350 women and children who had sought refuge there fought against 2,600 European Americans and 600 other American Indians. See also www.nps.gov/hobe.

The Liberty Bell: From Obscurity to Icon (36)

Analyzes the influences that shaped the bell's symbolic meanings, including for abolition of slavery and for women's rights. See also www.nps.gov/inde.

Federal/National

Californio to American: A Study in Cultural Change (8)

Californios (Spanish settlers) occupied the land of the Indian village of Puvungna, raised cattle, and built adobe houses on their cattle ranches. Over time, Rancho Los Alamitos became an elegant 19-room ranch house. National Register of Historic Places.

Hopewell Furnace: A Pennsylvania Iron-making Plantation (97)

A small if noisy village from its continually running iron furnaces, Hopewell was bound together in a common enterprise. Its 200-300 inhabitants lived near each other—the iron master, his wife and family, the workers and their families. The village also had a school. Some women worked in the ironmaster's Big House as domestic servants. Others did laundry, boarded single men, raised chickens and sold eggs, sold their baked goods and sewed, mended and washed clothing (arduous work when every gallon of water had to be fetched and heated, and the clothes boiled, beaten and rinsed). Village women grew family gardens and worked at harvest time, all contributing to the welfare of their families and their villages. See also www.nps.gov/hofu.

"The Great Chief Justice" at Home (49)

During the early 19th century, John Marshall—key U.S. Supreme Court justice—lived in this Richmond, Virginia, home with his wife Mary Willis Ambler—"my dearest Polly." Two symbolic items, his judicial robe worn as chief justice and a small locket that was worn by Marshall's wife, show the public and private man. National Historic Landmark.

Lincoln Boyhood National Memorial: Forging Greatness during Lincoln's Youth (126)

Here, from 1816-1830, young Abraham Lincoln lived on the Indiana frontier from age seven to 21. After he lost his mother Nancy Hanks Lincoln, his step-mother Sarah Bush Johnston, a widow with three of her own children, joined the family. Their frontier conditions prevented much schooling, but his famous love of books shaped his life. His mother and step-mother struggled with the primitive conditions their families endured. See also www.nps.gov/libo.

New Philadelphia: A Multiracial Town on the Illinois Frontier (130)

"Free Frank" McWorter married his wife Lucy in 1799 while they were still slaves; he purchased her freedom in 1817 and his own two years later. Because she was free, their son Squire was born free. (A mother's status—free or enslaved—determined her children's status.) Once free himself, Frank McWorter could own property; he purchased land in Kentucky. But living in Kentucky as a slave state was risky, so they moved and founded New Philadelphia in the Illinois territory, a once "bustling" town. By his 1854 death, "Free Frank" McWorter had been married 55 years and had purchased the freedom of 16 of his enslaved family members. National Historic Landmark.

The Trail of Tears and the Forced Relocation of the Cherokee Nation (118)

In 1838, the forced removal began of Cherokees along with Choctaw, Chickasaw, Creek, and Seminole tribes from their southeastern homelands in parts of North Carolina, Tennessee, Georgia, and Alabama, to lands now in Oklahoma. The 100,000 American Indians forced from their homes included women and children, who traveled by land and water over 1000 miles. Only the sick, aged, children, and nursing mothers with infants rode in wagons. Many people died. The Trail of Tears commemorates this removal. A Cherokee survivor later recalled, "Long time we travel on way to new land. People feel bad when they leave Old Nation. Women cry and made sad wails. Children cry and many men cry, and all look sad like when friends die, but they say nothing and just put heads down and keep on go towards West. Many days pass and people die very much." See *Oklahoman* (April 7, 1929), cited in *John Ehle, Trail of Tears: The Rise and Fall of the Cherokee Nation* (New York: Doubleday, 1988), p. 358. See also Trail of Tears National Historic Trail, www.nps.gov/trte.

The Building of the Chesapeake and Ohio Canal (10)

Begun in 1828, during the nation's canal building era, this early American canal greatly improved access between the tidewater region and the Allegheny Mountains, opening that area to more settlement and commerce. An internal improvement project, the C & O Canal dramatically dropped shipping rates and eased travel along its 185-mile length until closed by floods in 1924. Boats traveled nine months a year, making 25 trips each year, pulled along by mules on a towpath. Lockkeepers and their families lived in the small stone houses next to the 74 locks, opening the gates to allow the canal boats to move through and be lifted or lowered. Lockkeepers sold garden produce, milk, and eggs to the canal boaters. Families lived on the canal boats, children growing up on them (tethers kept them from falling into the canal), women sometimes steering them. Boys and girls cared for and drove the mules that pulled the boats along with their loads of wheat, corn, flour, lumber, and coal. Canal boat women cared for their families (living in 12 foot by 12 foot cabins), cooking, washing, sewing—doing all the usual chores but on a moving boat. Widows ran boats themselves. See also www.nps.gov/choh and also *Chesapeake and Ohio Canal National Historic Park, National Park Service Handbook 142* (1991).

Martin Van Buren's "Return to the Soil" (39)

After the widowed Van Buren retired from the presidency to Lindenwald, New York, until his 1862 death, he lived in a world of family who joined him there and of Irish servants, single women refugees from the potato famine and Irish families who had arrived earlier. See also www.nps.gov/mava; for servants on the website, see Patricia West, "Irish Immigrant Workers in Antebellum New York: The Experience of Domestic Servants at Van Buren's Lindenwald."

Mid to Late 19th Century

The Old Court House in St. Louis: Yesterday & Today (9)

Here Dred Scott—and his wife Harriet Scott (d. 1876)—fought for their freedom from slavery in this courthouse—and lost. Beginning in 1846, they sued for their freedom, arguing that, because they had spent time in free states (Illinois and Minnesota), they should be free themselves. Eventually in 1857, in the U.S. Supreme Court ruled against them; slaves were property and not U.S. citizens—the *Dred Scott* decision hastened the American Civil War. In May 1858 the Scotts, freed by their owners separately from the court decision, registered as free people. See also www.nps.gov/jeff and Donald Dosch, *The Old Courthouse* (St. Louis: Jefferson National Expansion Historical Association, 1979). See also www.nps.gov/jeff.

Building America's Industrial Revolution:
The Boott Cotton Mills of Lowell, Massachusetts (21)

Textile mills revolutionized American industry, changing many lives, especially the young women who left New England's farms for the mills and the later immigrants—Irish, French-Canadian, Greeks, Polish, and Portuguese—who also found work there. Lowell, the first large, planned, industrial city in America, harnessed the Pawtucket Falls's 32-foot drop into six miles of canals that provided energy to run the 40 mills—in the 1820s, the latest technology. With its many factories, the city of Lowell grew from 2,500 to 33,000 residents. Initially its owners provided schools, churches, libraries, and housing for their "mill girls," who published the famous *Lowell Offering*. These women lived in company boarding houses, their lives carefully regulated but with opportunities such as libraries and literary circles greater than in farming villages. After paying their expenses, the "mill girls" could save. As historian Thomas Dublin explains, "[She] quite likely had more ready cash than her father. It was common for young women to return home after a year in the mills with $25-$50 in a bank account." In 1836 and other years, Lowell workers protested various work requirement increases. By the 1850s, 10,000 workers labored six days per week to turn cotton into finished cloth. Cotton cloth increased demand for raw cotton, expanding

African American slavery to grow more cotton. Labor conditions deteriorated during the following decades; workers struck in 1903 and 1912. By the 1920s, the Lowell mills closed as new textile plants opened in the South. For more information, see also www.nps.gov/lowe. For Dublin quote, see *Lowell: The Story of an Industrial City National Park Handbook 140* (1992), p. 40.

First Battle of Manassas: An End to Innocence (12)

On Sunday, July 21, 1861, the elderly Mrs. Judith Carter Henry, her daughter Ellen, and a "hired [black] girl," Lucy Griffith, were living at Spring Hill Farm. Her sons looked after them. When the battle of First Manassas and cannon fire came near, her family wanted to move the aged and bedridden Mrs. Henry to greater safety. But she insisted on staying in her own bed. Her house soon became part of the battlefield. A shell shattered her bed; she was thrown to the floor—now wounded in her neck, side, and with one foot partly blown off. She died later that day, another casualty of the American Civil War. See also www.nps.gov/mana.

The Battle of Bentonville: Caring for Casualties of the Civil War (69)

By 1859, John and Amy Harper built a new, two-story frame home for their growing family of nine children. When the Civil War began two years later, one son enlisted in the Confederate army. In spring 1865, the war came home to Arkansas as the Battle of Bentonville was fought a mile away and Union surgeons took over their home as a field hospital. The family took refuge upstairs while surgeons operated downstairs, "cutting off arms and legs and throwing them out of the windows where they lay scattered on the grass." In the horror, the Harper family refused to leave their home. Afterwards, wounded Union soldiers were taken elsewhere, but 45 wounded Confederate soldiers remained. Their son later remembered that his parents had been "nurses, surgeons, commissaries, chaplains and undertakers. My mother fed them, washed their wounds, pointed them to the Saviour, closed their eyes when all was over, and helped to bury their uncoffined bodies as tenderly as she could." The family buried the nineteen soldiers who died from their wounds there. National Historic Landmark.

Chatham Plantation: Witness to the Civil War (45)

On the Rappahannock River, just across from Fredericksburg, Virginia, Chatham plantation life changed dramatically with the Civil War. In 1861, Mr. J. Horace Lacy joined the Confederate army while his wife and their five children moved away from their home, expecting battles there. They moved their household goods and their slaves further south. In 1865, at the end of the war, they returned and found their home uninhabitable. The area had indeed seen battles there, and the house had been severely damaged. Mrs. Lacy called it "heartrending" as paneling had been stripped from the walls, and doors and windows were gone—"and there were nineteen Federal graves on the lawn." No one recorded the thoughts from the people once enslaved there. See also www.nps.gov/frsp, which includes a letter from Clara Barton while there.

The Old Mormon Fort: Birthplace of Las Vegas, Nevada (122)

Helen Stewart (1854-1926) played a key role in the early history of the city of Las Vegas, which began as a Mormon mission in 1855 before becoming a cattle ranch. Her husband Archibald Stewart acquired the ranch, planning to raise horses, cattle, and crops on it. Thirty-eight years old, he had a successful freighting business in Nevada. In California in 1872, he met and married then 18-year-old Helen Wiser. Later, he decided to move to his Nevada ranch. Helen Stewart moved reluctantly, wanting a more established community with schooling for their children. They arrived in Las Vegas in April 1882 with their three children; she had a fourth child soon after they arrived. Stewart promised his family they would only stay in Las Vegas two years. But before the two years was over, a neighbor killed Archibald Stewart. Helen Stewart buried her husband in a coffin made from the doors of their house. Weeks later, she gave birth to their son Archibald, named after his father. With the help of foremen and her father, she operated the ranch and bought large tracts of land, hoping that the railroad would come to the Las Vegas valley. The railroad did. It wanted the ranch's water for its steam-powered locomotives and beef for its workers. In 1902, she sold the ranch for $55,000—an enormous sum—and bought another one. Three years later, the railroad sold her ranch off as city lots for the new town of Las Vegas, Nevada. Stewart supported education for Las Vegas and Paiute Indian children. Paiutes had been her friends, companions, and helpers throughout her adult life. Helen Stewart became the first woman elected to Clark County School Board, the first woman to sit on a jury in Nevada, and Las Vegas's first postmaster from 1893-1903. She died in 1926. National Register of Historic Places.

The Penniman House: A Whaling Story (112)

In 1852, at age 21, Captain Edward Penniman sailed on his first whaling voyage, eventually sailing on seven voyages with New Bedford, Massachusetts, his home port. The captain sailed in the Arctic, Cape Verde Islands, Panama, New Zealand, Hawaii, and elsewhere around the globe. Not liking being alone on the three to four year whaling voyages, he took his family with him. They sometimes brought their two sons and a daughter as well. On the ship, his wife Betsy Augusta Penniman— "Gustie"—cared for her family, teaching their children and actively participating in the whaling expeditions. She once sailed the ship 100 miles during a storm to retrieve her husband the captain who had gone ashore. From their whaling voyage profits, they built the French Second Empire house that still stands on Cape Cod, Massachusetts. Its eight rooms were once filled with Arctic bear robes, paintings, scrimshaw, and other artifacts from around the world as well as the over 100 glass plate negatives their daughter Bessie Penniman took between 1880 and 1913. See also www.nps.gov/caco.

Locke and Walnut Grove: Havens for Early Asian Immigrants in California

Although immigration restrictions and their expectations of soon returning back home resulted in a predominantly male Chinese immigrant population, after the 1882 anti-Chinese legislation more Japanese came. Some Japanese men later brought their wives they had left behind in Japan to the U.S. Others married "picture brides"; families selected their sons' wives based solely on the women's photographs. These Japanese farm laborers built their families homes in a *nihonmachi*, or Japanese section of town. Walnut Grove is a National Historic District; Locke a National Historic Landmark.

Gilded Age/Progressive Era

Carnegie Libraries: The Future Made Bright (50)

Seeking a way to bring Americans (especially new immigrants) into an increasingly industrial and technological world and provide well-educated voters, the industrialist and philanthropist Andrew Carnegie paid for several thousand library buildings across the nation, greatly influencing their design as well. He believed that libraries provided people from all classes access to lifelong education. Women's clubs and the Women's Christian Temperance Union also raised money for these libraries, believing they offered men an alternative to drinking in saloons. Later, the emphasis changed to providing trained librarians, a profession found socially acceptable for women.

Chicago's Black Metropolis: Understanding History through a Historic Place (53)

This African American "city-within-a-city" prospered from the late 19th century until the 1930s during the height of the Jim Crow era that decreed public segregation between blacks and whites. Many cities with substantial black populations developed their own institutions, including churches, insurance companies, beauty parlors, barber shops, funeral parlors, clubs, and hotels. Here, Overton cosmetics provided beauty treatments for black women from the Overton Hygienic Building. (See Chicago Travel Itinerary for other sites.)

The Freeman School: Building Prairie Communities (80)

This late-19th-century one-room school in Nebraska formed the center of its farming community where both male and female students attended grades 1 to 6. Its female teachers provided these children a basic public education. Under portraits of George Washington and Abraham Lincoln, students learned to read, write, spell, and do arithmetic. They learned about their country and its values. The school house also served as a community center to this Midwestern farming community.

An American Success Story: The Pope House of Raleigh, North Carolina (124)

An African American family through several generations refused to accept second class treatment. From free black parentage, Dr. Manassa

Pope became an M.D. and politically active. His first wife died young. His second wife, Delia, a teacher before they married (married women were not allowed to be teachers), later became a cosmetics representative for the company owned by Madam C. J. Walker, a famous and successful black businesswoman who manufactured and sold beauty and hair products for African American women. One of the Pope daughters became a librarian at the African American North Carolina Central University Law School; the other, a home economics teacher in the Chapel Hill public schools. The daughters had careers much sought by middle-class black women, many of whom could only find work as maids or washerwomen.

Glen Echo Park: Center for Education and Recreation (24)

Initially built during the late 19th century, Glen Echo Park was part of the Chautauqua movement that provided "continuing education" to the public. During its Chautauqua days, sadly short because people thought there had been a malaria death there, the public participated in the following: "music (both vocal and instrumental), American history, languages (including Latin, French, German, and Hebrew), "The Care and Development of Physical Powers," "Methods for Secular Teachers," "Modern Poets," "English Authors," astronomy, geology, and Egyptology. The Chautauqua also offered evening band concerts, poetry readings, and dances. Later, Glen Echo Park became a Maryland amusement park at the end of a trolley line from Washington, D.C. Glen Echo became controversial for its racial segregation; it later integrated. See www.nps.gov/glec.

Gold Fever! Seattle Outfits the Klondike Gold Rush (55)

The discovery of gold in the Canada's remote Klondike region touched off a great gold rush, creating an economic boom that changed the city of Seattle forever. See www.nps.gov/klgo.

Iron Hill School: An African-American One-Room School (58)

Built in 1923 in rural Delaware, Iron Hill School was one of 80 elementary schools businessman and philanthropist Pierre Samuel du Pont built in his efforts to improve education for African American children. The simple but well-designed schools made education more accessible to black children living there. National Register of Historic Places.

Navesink Lighthouse and Robbins Reef Lighthouse: Lighting the Way through New York Bay (131)

Historic lighthouses show the technological advancements that increased maritime safety and the isolated, often routine, but sometimes heroic lives led by their keepers. In New York Bay, people still call Robbins Reef "Kate's Light." Kate Walker served as principal keeper at the isolated lighthouse from 1894 to 1919, although government regulations did not allow women to be *in charge of* offshore lighthouses. (Many women were assistant lighthouse keepers.) She retired after 19 years, having raised two children and rescued some 50 people. When asked about her difficult, isolated, and dangerous life, she replied, "It isn't much of a story. Just keep the light burning and the fog-bell wound up and the siren ready all the time. That's all." See William Hemmingway, "The Woman of the Light," *Harper's Weekly*, 14 August 1909, p. 11. National Historic Landmark.

Run For Your Lives! The Johnstown Flood of 1889 (5)

A flood caused by poorly maintained dams 14 miles upstream killed 2,200 people in this Pennsylvania town of 30,000. Those people who survived had horrific accounts of flood and then fire as enormous piles of flood debris burned, killing more victims. Clara Barton, founder and president of the American Red Cross, worked for months helping its victims, building "hotels" for the homeless, and proving her newly-formed organization's usefulness in disasters. See also www.nps.gov/jofl.

Skagway: Gateway to the Klondike (75)

With the 1898 stampede for gold, over 100,000 prospectors set out for the Klondike—including some women also eager for riches. Most did not succeed. See also www.nps.gov/klgo.

Springwood: Birthplace and Home to Franklin D. Roosevelt (82)

His mother Sara Roosevelt's home as much as President Roosevelt's, this mansion first helped shape FDR's worldview. Later his wife Eleanor Roosevelt lived there as well; FDR built her Val-Kill as her own home and retreat and built his own nearby Top Cottage. As his widow explained in 1946, "Life here had always a healing quality for him." See also www.nps.gov/hofr and www.nps.gov/elro.

Ybor City: Cigar Capital of the World (51)

Immigrant cigar makers—both women and men—in Tampa, Florida, adapted to life in the U.S. life in the late 19th and early 20th century while maintaining their ethnic identity. Here, they made high quality cigars, skillfully wrapping tobacco leaves together to make them. Readers—"lectors"—often read newspapers and classic novels to these often illiterate but well-informed artisans as they worked. The cigar makers also frequented mutual aid societies that provided them with various services as well as a strong ethnic community. Because so many of the cigar makers were Cuban (although many other nationalities lived there) who supported Cuba's freedom from Spain, many contributed to the revolutionary cause. National Register of Historic Places.

Early to Mid 20th Century

Birthplace of John F. Kennedy: Home of the Boy Who Would Be President (33)

Rose Kennedy, his mother, was matriarch of the Kennedy family whose members have so influenced this nation's history. He grew up in this home in Brookline, Massachusetts. See also www.nps.gov/jofi.

Harry Truman and Independence, Missouri: "This is where I belong" (103)

Harry and Bess Truman lived in her family's home, making it their own. Known as unpretentious, they preferred their quiet study full of books and music room to the politics of Washington, D.C. Asked what she wanted to do after her husband's Presidency ended, she replied, "Return to Independence." See also www.nps.gov/hstr.

Herbert Hoover: Iowa Farm Boy and World Humanitarian (34)

Born in a village in Iowa and orphaned as a child, Hoover went west. Both Hoover and his wife Lou Henry Hoover were educated at Stanford University and became geologists. Working in Australia and China as a mining engineer, he grew wealthy. He became recognized internationally for his work alleviating the malnutrition of Belgian children during World War I. He served as Secretary of Commerce under Presidents Harding and Coolidge. Elected president in 1928, he struggled to respond to the economic crisis that became the Great Depression. West Branch, Iowa, preserves and interprets his small birthplace cottage, the Friends Meeting House, his father's blacksmith shop, and related buildings. See also www.nps.gov/heho.

Paterson, New Jersey: America's Silk City (102)

In the 1880s, Paterson or "Silk City" produced nearly half the silk cloth manufactured in the U.S. Its skilled workforce, mostly immigrants, almost half women, spent their work lives in the silk mills, handling the delicate threads and making them into fabrics. Labor relationships were also delicate: between 1881 and 1900, Paterson had nearly 140 strikes, both reflecting tensions and resulting in a decreased work week of "only" 55 hours. But in January 1913, 800 weavers, angry at increased workloads, walked off their jobs, soon joined by other workers and by key labor organizers from the IWW (Industrial Workers of the World, better known as the "Wobblies"), including the famous labor organizer Elizabeth Gurley Flynn. By February, 300 mills had closed and 24,000 workers had joined the industry-wide strike; over 2,000 workers were arrested. But by May 1913 the owners won, and the IWW lost its dominance. Interestingly, the strike had little violence (unlike places such as Ludlow, Colorado, where strikers' families were killed). As organizer Big Bill Haywood told the workers, "Your power is in your folded arms. . . . You have killed the mills; you have stopped production; you have broken off the profits. Any other violence you may commit is less than this, and it will only react upon yourselves." See Frederick S. Boyd, "The General Strike in the Silk Industry," in *The Pageant of the Paterson Strike* (New York: Success Press, 1913), p. 5.

Pietro Botto, a northern Italian immigrant, worked in the silk mills; his wife Maria Botto worked at home as a "picker," a skilled worker who examined finished fabric for flaws. By 1907, they had built a house near Paterson, living in its first floor and renting out the upstairs. On a typical Sunday, wife Maria Botto and their daughters cooked for as many as 100 visitors. Strike organizers used their home's second-floor balcony, allowing IWW leaders to hold rallies there for the striking workers, encouraging the workers' morale during the months-long strike. Organizer Elizabeth Gurley Flynn later remembered, "We spoke to the strikers Sunday after Sunday. . . . We spoke to enormous crowds of thousands of people—the strikers and their families, workers from other Paterson industries, people from New Jersey cities, delegations from New York, trade unionists, students and others . . . from all over America and from foreign countries." World War I and eventually synthetic silk (rayon) ended Paterson's dominance. See Elizabeth Gurley Flynn, *The Rebel Girl, My First Life: 1906-1926* (New York: International Publishers, 1973), p. 165; cited in James Sheire, "Pietro Botto House" (Passaic County, New Jersey) National Historic Landmark Documentation, Washington, D.C.: U.S. Department of the Interior, National Park Service, 1982, Section 8, p. 15.

The War Relocation Centers of World War II: When Fear Was Stronger than Justice (89)

Fearful that they might help the Japanese enemy, in 1942 the U.S. government issued Executive Order 9066 that sent nearly 120,000 people of Japanese ethnicity to relocation centers in very remote areas of this country. Forced from their homes, farms and work, these men, women and children—many of them U.S. citizens—took only what few possessions they could carry with them to these desolate camps with their flimsy barracks and daily humiliations. In spite of their families' internments, some Japanese men enlisted as soldiers to fight for the U.S., and some Japanese women volunteered for the Women's Army Corps and the American Red Cross. Other Japanese women left the camps for colleges and jobs, shifting away from the domestic service jobs they had before World War II into nursing, clerical, and other positions. See Valerie Matsumoto, "Japanese American Women during World War II" in *Unequal Sisters: A Multicultural Reader in U.S. Women's History*, Vicki Ruiz and Ellen DuBois, eds., 3rd edition (New York: Routledge, 2000).

Mid to Late 20th Century

Brown v. Board: Five Communities That Changed America (121)

Linda Brown's father wanted his African American daughter to attend a well equipped and supplied school in Topeka, Kansas—with white students. He did not want her to attend a segregated, poorly furnished school. His legal case and five others joined together to form the famous 1954 *Brown v. Board of Education* Supreme Court decision that overturned earlier legal decisions that "separate but equal" educational facilities were constitutional. See also www.nps.gov/brvb.

New Kent School and the George W. Watkins School: From Freedom of Choice to Integration (104)

Schools had been legally segregated since the 1896 *Plessy v. Ferguson* Supreme Court decision. In 1954, the Court decided that separate meant unequal and so overturned its earlier decision. But most southern schools remained strictly segregated, having been told to desegregate only "with all deliberate speed"—a vague standard that allowed local opponents to prevent white and black children from going to school together. New Kent County, Virginia, had two schools, one white, one black, the black school with dedicated teachers but inadequate resources.

The New Kent School and the George W. Watkins School, located in New Kent County, Virginia, gave rise to the key 1968 Supreme Court decision that directed schools boards to integrate their schools with black and white children attending classes together. White "massive resistance" and other efforts to thwart public school integration were now declared unconstitutional. Photographs of students in the two schools "tell" the story. So does the oral history interview of African American Cynthia Lewis Gaines, former George W. Watkins school student and one of the first students to integrate a New Kent School, under "freedom of choice." During her first year, no white students sat next to her, and she suffered various torments. But her next year, she gained some white friends.

The Selma to Montgomery Voting Rights March: Shaking the Conscience of the Nation (133)

On Sunday night, March 7, 1965, Alabama state troopers attacked 600 African men and women demonstrators peacefully marching 54 miles from Selma, Alabama, to the state's capital, Montgomery, demanding their voting rights. As they tried to cross the Pettus Bridge, police with batons, tear gas and horses attacked them, sending many to hospitals with broken limbs, concussions and causing one leader, Hosea Williams, to ask, "Oh my god, how many people did I lead to their death today?" Selma resident Amelia Boynton and her friend Marie Foster, long time activists, were in the front: "I didn't think anything was going to happen," she remembered. She had her high heel shoes on. Beaten at the bridge, she was taken to a funeral home but revived a few hours later.

Decades of NAACP legal efforts to get black voting rights had been stymied; a younger black generation frustrated with the slow pace of blacks being allowed to vote chose non-violent but highly visible tactics instead. They effectively used television images to show the rest of the country the actual conditions Southern blacks encountered. White Southerners who wanted to keep the power structure as it had long been unleashed brutal fury against blacks who wanted their political rights as American citizens. The Civil Rights Act of 1964 had become law a year earlier, and the summer of 1964 had seen massive voter registration efforts. But myriad tactics had long kept blacks from actually registering to vote—much less voting. "Literacy tests" failed blacks on whims. President Lyndon B. Johnson was furious. On March 15, speaking to a televised joint session of Congress (long before CNN had been imagined) he forcefully said, "Their cause must be our cause too. Because it is not just Negroes, but really it is all of us who must overcome the crippling legacy of bigotry and injustice. And we shall overcome."

On Sunday, March 21, they marched again, "a holy crusade" determined to succeed. This time 7,000 protesters, black and white, men and women, formed an orderly procession with protection from the National Guard. This time they did.

Hosea Williams, John Lewis (then head of the Student Non-Violent Coordinating Committee, now a Congressman from Georgia), and Martin Luther King Jr. get justifiable credit for their bravery and leadership. Women get much less credit. Black women such as Marie Foster and Amelia Boynton who also risked their lives and livelihoods, women less frequently interviewed, their names still less known. Yet they were the backbone of the communities that built the civil rights movement and every bit as much involved. For example, Marie Foster, long active in the Dallas County Voters League, explained, "I called Amelia Boynton [and] we met the 23rd day of January, 1963. I said, 'Well how about this, let's start a citizenship class,'" trying to help blacks to pass the "literacy" tests. They did, helping black Americans register to vote. In 1965, some of the famous women quilters of Gee's Bend joined the second Selma march. They also took the ferry to go to their Camden County courthouse to register to vote. All the women were jailed; other retribution soon followed. Ferry service (road access was almost impossible) abruptly ended, homes bulldozed, and people suddenly fired.

No direct line existed from the laws and customs of Jim Crow segregation and intimidation to the 1965 Voting Rights Act. That was only one more step towards racial equality. Thousands and thousands of little incidents accumulated into larger ones, private ones into very public events. But the modern civil rights movement had taken another step towards its goals. Today, the route is a National Historic Trail, but the miles between Selma and Montgomery, Alabama, remain a haunted landscape. See also www.nps.gov/semo. All quotes from Teaching with Historic Places lesson plan *The Selma to Montgomery Voting Rights March: Shaking the Conscience of the Nation (133)*. For more information, see Lynne Olson, *Freedom's Daughters: The Unsung Heroines of the Civil Rights Movement from 1830 to 1970* (New York: Simon & Schuster, 2001); Paul Arnett, Joanne Cubbs, and Eugene W. Metcalf, Jr., eds., *Gee's Bend: The Architecture of the Quilt* (Atlanta: Tinwood Books, 2006) pp. 18-19.

Traveling: Women in Tours and Travel Itineraries (Going There!)

Tours

- Corbett, Cathy. *A Guide to St. Louis Women's History*. St. Louis: Missouri Historical Society Press, 1999.

- Kaufman, Polly. *Boston Women's Heritage Trail: A Self-Guided Walk through Four Centuries of Boston Women's History*. Boston: Boston Women's Heritage Trail, 2006.

- Kreuter, Gretchen. *Women's History Tours of the Twin Cities*. Cambridge, Minn.: Adventure Publications, 2008.

- Samuels, Gayle Brandow. *Women in the City of Brotherly Love, and Beyond: Tours and Detours in Delaware Valley Women's History*. n.p., 1996.

Travel Itineraries

National Park Service Travel Itineraries: Finding Women . . . across the U.S.A. http://www.nps.gov/history/nr/travel/index.htm or www.nps.gov "History and Culture," "For Travelers" and then "Travel Itineraries."

Special thanks to the National Register of Historic Places, National Park Service, Washington, D.C., and its partners for these itineraries. We have condensed their text and identified those places that specifically include women's history.

The National Park Service On-Line Travel Itineraries provide both "virtual visitors" and in-person ones with a rich variety of themes, and sites within those themes. Based on the 80,000 properties listed on the National Register of Historic Places, the Travel Itineraries are impressive. They are a rich but challenging resource for women's history. Frequently they reflect outdated history: mythical and royal women get recognition while other entries obscure girls' and women's presence even though other sources show them there. At the same time real gems also exist. Greater awareness may resolve these issues. The Museum Management sections have some excellent examples of women's history.

Only two of the several dozen travel itineraries specifically feature women: the 75-site New York and Massachusetts Itinerary "Places Where Women Made History" (don't they everywhere?) and the "World War II in the San Francisco Bay Area" site, which features an informative essay "Tending the Home Front: The Many Roles of Bay Area Women during World War II" by historian Donna Graves.

Many travel itineraries list numerous residences with wives and other females mentioned, usually in minor roles. Other sites omit key women. The "Richmond Itinerary" omits the St. Luke Building, headquarters of the African American women's Independent Order of St. Luke that Maggie Walker led. Sites that deeply affected women's lives ignore those effects, from water treatment plants (decreased disease) to railroads and canals (easier travel). "Finding" women requires reading every site listed, aided by knowledge of women's history. The American Presidents travel itinerary covers the first ladies, discussing their influences on fashion and their favorite recipes.

Too often, women's past gets inadequate recognition. Homes—occupied by several generations—often name only the males. For example, The Old Stone House entry in the Washington, D.C., tour credits Christopher Lehman and slights another longtime owner, Mrs. Cassandra Chew. Several families owned and ran Boston's Union Oyster House—presumably including women; many lighthouse keepers' families worked to fulfill the duties required to keep shipping safe; women became assistant lighthouse keepers as well. Where were they? Sites that profoundly *affected* women's lives often omit those impacts. A great deal of emphasis is given to the (female named) *ships* but little on the effects of men's long absences and New England port populations becoming heavily female. See Elaine Forman Crane, *Ebb Tide in New England: Women, Seaports, and Social Change, 1630-1800* (Boston: Northeastern Press, 1998).

In the Cumberland, Maryland, tour, improving city streets and sanitation—a major Progressive goal often championed by women's groups—solely credits Mayor Thomas Koon, implying no women were active there. If women were active there, no recognition is given. Greater historical context provides greater present understanding. Analyses that highlight women's changing roles from producers to consumers tell us more than those that focus solely on changes in merchandising and the emergence of department stores.

In addition to those sites listed below, NPS travel itineraries include even more sites associated with women's history. More research will add even more women's history sites to the list. Women's history is everywhere—just look for it.

Aboard the Underground Railroad

- Homes, churches, and businesses of abolitionists and former slaves.
- Prudence Crandall in 1833 opened a school for "young misses of color" in Canterbury, Connecticut, later closed down.
- Harriet Beecher Stowe, author of *Uncle Tom's Cabin*, had homes in Cincinnati, Ohio; Brunswick, Maine; and Hartford, Connecticut.
- Abolitionists Samuel and Sally Wilson's home in Cincinnati, Ohio, ran a station on the Underground Railroad there, helping fugitive slaves.

- Liberty Farm, in Worcester, Massachusetts, home of Abby Kelley Foster, outspoken abolitionist and early suffragist, and her husband, Stephen Symonds Foster, from 1847 until 1881.
- Friends Meeting House in Wilmington, Delaware, helped many slaves escape through Delaware into the free state of Pennsylvania.
- Mary Ann Shadd Cary, a writer, educator, lawyer, abolitionist, and the first North American black newspaperwoman, later lived in this Washington, D.C., brick row house. An outspoken and articulate abolitionist, she promoted equality for all people.
- Barney and Julia Ford home. Freed slaves who moved to Colorado in 1860 became wealthy, owning hotels, hair salons, barbershops, and restaurants.

Amana, Iowa

In this utopian German colony located in Iowa, life roles were strictly gendered. Their lifestyles, from 19th-century communal kitchens and dining to the 21st-century appliances that today make American dining much easier, provide a secondary but significant story to their original religious purpose. Begun as a German radical pietist sect in 1714, the Community of True Inspiration immigrated to the U.S. in 1842 to escape religious persecution. Like other pietist groups, they emphasized believers' personal religious experiences with God clearly working and speaking through his followers. Individuals who received these messages were *Werkzeuge* (instruments). Two *Werkzeuge* lived in the Amana Colonies: Christian Metz (1794-1867) and Barbara Heinemann Landmann (1795-1883), the last *Werkzeug*. The church continues today as the Amana Church Society.

By the 1860s, Amana Colony had seven villages on over 20,000 acres of land. Their brick dwellings reflect their residents' deliberately simple lives. Each person in the village was assigned a residence, with three to four families (often related by kinship or marriage) sharing each one. Several generations of one family lived together in one dwelling. Most women, starting around 14 years, worked in the communal kitchens and gardens. Women also did laundry, sewing, and knitting. A few women worked in the community's main industry, their woolen mills. (Men's jobs were far more varied.) Each Amana village had a *Kinderschule* for children ages two to seven. (Mothers stayed with their children until age two before returning to their village assignments.) Children attended school from ages of seven to 14. At age 14, the community sent girls to kitchen assignments and boys to farms, shops or mills. At the kitchens, men and women ate separately with little conversation. Each kitchen had a *Küchebaas* (kitchen boss) who directed meal preparation. She lived in an adjoining house with her family and also supervised the essential food-producing gardens and food preservation.

By the 1930s, many community members found the communal rules that governed everything, including dress, dining, and recreation, to be petty and overly restrictive. Young people wanted to play baseball, to own musical instruments, or girls to bob their hair in the new style. Families wanted to eat at home together. The Amana Society had lost an important source of revenue when its calico print works, which had once produced 4500 yards daily, making fabrics women wore, closed after World War I. In 1931, the community had a choice: return to a "more austere and disciplined life" or abandon the communal system. They chose the latter. The Amana colonies split into the community and the corporation, with the Amana Church still central to its community. The corporation produces domestic appliances under the Amana brand–the refrigerators, freezers, and microwaves that have revolutionized American cooking overwhelmingly done by American women. Today a large, now private, plant produces these appliances as well as air conditioners; the 19th-century woolen mill smokestack still rises over Amana's modern plant.

Amistad: Seeking Freedom in Connecticut

Three African girls were on the slave ship *Amistad* when it was taken over by its African captives in this famous defiance of enslavement.

American Presidents

Since most of the presidents were married (Van Buren was a widower), their wives and families both accompanied them to the White House and came and returned to their own homes. These homes often can be used as snapshots of different times and periods, from the very simple birth homes of Abraham Lincoln and Herbert Hoover to the mansions of Theodore Roosevelt and Woodrow Wilson, with the comfortable but very nice homes of the Eisenhowers and John F. Kennedy (JFK) birthplace in between. With its Victorian furnishings, the Andrew Johnson home in Johnson City, Tennessee, served as his family's home before and after his presidency. Presidential sites also include special places, such as Herbert and Lou Henry Hoovers' Rapidan Camp in Shenandoah National Park and Theodore Roosevelt's very simple cabin in Theodore Roosevelt National Park in North Dakota. The Hoovers fished and relaxed at the Rapidan Camp; Theodore Roosevelt grieved for his wife and mother and played at being a cowboy in North Dakota before returning to politics with his characteristic energy. Years later, TR used his porch at Sagamore Hill to promote women's suffrage. Woodrow Wilson's home in Washington, D.C., sheltered him after his stroke, with his wife Edith Galt Wilson caring for him and the nation as well. The Adams home in Massachusetts housed John Adams, his amazing wife Abigail Adams, their son John Quincy Adams, and other family members. Here, she kept the family farming business profitable so that her husband could work for the young country. Betty and Gerald Ford moved from their Alexandria, Virginia, home into the White House when he became president after President Nixon resigned. Their post-World War II suburban home well reflects that time; a picture shows him cooking in the house's kitchen. Other properties associated with presidents have been so changed that they show relatively little of their residents' lives and characters.

Many of the presidents also have National Historic Sites or National Monuments. The best way to access these sites is to go to www.nps.gov and search for individual parks there. See also their websites for more about them and their wives, families, and the other women in their lives. Lincoln birthplace is www.nps.gov/abli; his boyhood home is www.nps.gov/libo; Hoover birthplace is www.nps.gov/heho; Theodore Roosevelt's birthplace is www.nps.gov/thrb, his Sagamore Hill home is www.nps.gov/sahi; Woodrow Wilson's home, a National Trust for Historic Preservation property in Washington, D.C., is www.woodrowwilsonhouse.org; Eisenhower's home is www.nps.gov/eise; JFK birthplace is www.nps.gov/jofi; Andrew Johnson's home (and tailor shop where his wife read to her then-illiterate husband) is www.nps.gov/anjo. The Adams National Historical Park (www.nps.gov/adam) tells the story of four generations of the Adams family (1720 to 1927). Abigail Smith Adams, a self-educated woman (no schools were open to girls then) had a long, happy, and strong marriage to John Adams as he moved from young lawyer to revolutionary to president; their son John Quincy Adams also became president. "Exceptionally capable of managing the family finances and household," she served on the American Revolutionary home front (she watched the Battle of Bunker Hill from her home) through very difficult times. Anti-slavery, she argued for rights of both women and blacks to her husband—unsuccessfully then. Abigail Adams' role in supporting her husband needs greater recognition. The Ford home in Alexandria, Virginia, is a National Historic Landmark. Nixon's birthplace and library is www.nixonlibraryfoundation.org.

American Southwest

• San Juan Pueblo, first visited by Europeans in 1541, remains home to Hopi people today. They are known for their one- and two-story square adobe houses and the Oke Owinge Arts and Crafts Cooperative, famous for its exquisite pottery. A circa 1906 photograph shows women and children there.

• Old Governor's Mansion/Sharlot Hall Museum, a large one-and one-half story rustic log building from 1864, served as the home of the Territorial Governor and hall for the Arizona Territorial Government before becoming home to State Historian Sharlot Hall. (Arizona gained its statehood in 1912).

• Wheelwright Museum of the American Indian. Together, Mary Cabot Wheelwright (1878-1958) and Hastiin Klah (1867-1937), a highly respected Navajo medicine man, collected and preserved Navajo religious ceremonial artifacts and recordings. In 1937, she built this Santa Fe, New Mexico, museum to preserve and interpret these key and endangered cultural artifacts.

• Best known as a trapper and a mountain man, Kit Carson served as an army guide, Indian Agent, and highly celebrated Army officer during the Indian Wars. He was also a husband and father, marrying an Arapahoe Indian woman Waa-nibe (Singing Grass). After she died, Kit Carson moved to Taos, marrying Josefa Jaramillo from a prominent Hispanic family. Although he was 33 years old when she was 14 years old, their happy marriage lasted 25 years with seven children. Their one-story adobe house, built in 1825 in the Spanish Colonial style, has nine rooms surrounding an open patio with a well. Their home shows a different side of Kit Carson and an important frontier family.

• Founded in 1878, and now the oldest continuously operating trading post on the Navajo Reservation, Hubbell Trading Post linked Navajo weavers and silversmiths with markets and played a key role on the Navajo reservation as both a business and community place. John Lorenzo Hubbell, son of an Anglo American and a Hispanic woman, married Lena Rubi. Their four children included Barbara, who served as Ganado's postmistress for many years, and Roman, whose second wife Dorothy first came to New Mexico to teach the Hubbell children and grandchildren after his first wife had died in the 1918 great flu epidemic. Long ill, Roman Hubbell died in 1957. For the next eight years, Dorothy Smith Hubbell operated and preserved the post until it became a National Historic Site. See also www.nps.gov/hutr.

Asheville, North Carolina

• Ottari Sanitarium and Highland Hospitals treated tuberculosis patients from all over when consumption killed many people.

• Princess Anne Hotel, founded by nurse Anne O'Connell in 1922, housed families of tuberculosis patients being treated at nearby boarding houses, hotels, and resorts.

• Grove Park Inn hosted mountain visitors, including Eleanor Roosevelt, while other tourists stayed at the Brexton Boarding House, originally operated as a tuberculosis sanitarium by Roman Catholic Sisters of Mercy nuns

Ashland, Oregon

• Emil and Alice Applegate Peil House, home of the area's first female school principal. She was also important in developing the Chautauqua, Ashland Library, and the Oregon Shakespeare Festival. She was "an active partner" in the Peil Implement Company, which manufactured wagon and agricultural implements.

• Ahlstrom House, whose owners "Nils and his [unnamed] wife buried five of their small children after a diphtheria epidemic."

• Peerless Rooms Building, housing built in 1904 by Oscar and Lucinda Ganiard, who built many commercial buildings in Ashland.

• Women's Civic Improvement Clubhouse, built as part of the Progressive era of civic pride and social functions; it housed meetings, banquets, and shows.

Atlanta, Georgia

• Herndon Home of Alonzo Herndon, who founded the Atlanta Life Insurance Company, becoming Atlanta's first black millionaire. Adrienne Herndon, his first wife and a teacher at Atlanta University, did its primary design.

- Fulton Bag and Cotton Mill. During the late 19th century, its owners built employee housing, from shotgun cottages to bungalows, in "Cabbagetown."
- Sweet Auburn Historic District, birthplace to the martyred Rev. Dr. Martin Luther King Jr., the civil rights leader and minister, now part of Martin Luther King National Historic Site. In 1974, his mother was shot and killed as she played the organ at its Ebenezer Baptist Church.
- Gladys Knight sang at the Royal Peacock Club there.
- Apartment where Margaret Mitchell wrote *Gone with the Wind*.

Aviation: From Sand Dunes to Sonic Booms

- Atchison, Kansas, birthplace of Amelia Earhart, the first woman to fly solo across the Atlantic Ocean in 1932, the U.S., and California to Hawaii. She later disappeared on a long distance flight.
- Marjorie Stinson, who founded and operated the Stinson School of Aviation in 1916 in San Antonio, Texas.

Baltimore, Maryland

- The Johns Hopkins Hospital Complex, built 1877-1889, housed both the first formal medical school to admit women students and a major nursing school.
- Mother Seton House. She founded the Sisters of Charity (a Roman Catholic Order) and a girls' school; first American woman saint.
- St. Mary's Chapel where the Oblate Sisters of Providence, an order of black nuns founded in the late 1820s, used the Chapel basement to teach black children.
- Eastern Female High School, founded 1844, provided early high school education to girls; in 1904, a Campfire Girls founder attended there.
- Fells Point, an 18th- to 19th-century residential community for maritime workers and their families.

Cane River National Heritage Area (Northwest Louisiana)

- Marie Thérèse Coincoin's home (Maison de Marie Thérèse), a Creole-style cottage. An African American woman whose French partner freed her and their children before he married a French woman in 1786, she became a successful tobacco planter herself. "Her home" was probably built after her death.
- Caspiana Plantation Store, built in 1906, where African American workers purchased their staples and goods from white landowners under the "crop lien" system, which only increased their indebtedness year by year.
- Women's gymnasium, Northwestern State University, built in 1930s with a dance studio, gym, and walking track. Physical education then became an academic major.
- Melrose Plantation, where famed "self-taught" African American artist Clementine Hunter began painting haunting images and where

Cammie Garrett Henry started an art colony that hosted author William Faulkner and other southern authors.

- Kate Chopin House, where she and her husband Oscar Chopin lived in Cloutierville in 1879, inspired her two novels, *At Fault* and *The Awakening*.

Chicago, Illinois

Historic properties mention "office spaces and shops" in the Rookery and the arts scene in the Auditorium Building but without any discussion those who *worked or performed* in those places—presumably some women were involved. Descriptions here include very little evidence of women, even though department stores and mail order firms greatly affected women's lives and consumer choices. Domestic architecture barely mentions families living in these homes.

- Montgomery Ward and Company Building. Since 1909, the Montgomery Ward and Company complex along the Chicago River has served as national headquarters for the country's oldest mail order firm. The two earliest buildings, the old Administration Building and the Mail Order House, still remain. Mail order business opened up consumer choice to families living far from towns and cities and also sold better goods at better prices, greatly affecting women's lives.

- Reid Murdoch Building, designed in 1913-1914, was constructed as a food processing company and warehouse.

- Marshall Field Building. Marshall Field and Company built their third department store in 1892 (fires damaged their first two), which grew to occupy an entire city block in the city's emerging retail district. Field, a leading figure in the development of the department store, emphasized customer service, an important aspect of the greater American consumer economy and culture focused on women.

- Carson, Pirie, Scott and Company Building, commercial architecture that remains a department store. Other properties in the itinerary mention "office spaces and shops" in the Rookery, and the arts scene in the Auditorium Building but lack any discussion at all of those people who worked or performed in those places—presumably some women were there as artists, office workers, saleswomen, and customers.

- The Overton Hygienic Building housed African American Anthony Overton's banking, publishing, and cosmetics sales for black women that all responded to Jim Crow-era restrictions and segregation.

- Chicago Bee Building where African American entrepreneur Anthony Overton moved his cosmetic company after he had to vacate his own building in 1931. This building also has apartments.

- Frederick C. Robie House, built in 1909, affected residential architecture for many decades. In its May 1957 issue, *House and Home* magazine declared that "no house in America during the past hundred years matches the importance of Frank Lloyd Wright's Robie House." One of Frank Lloyd Wright's strongest Prairie House-style modern homes, it has free-flowing interior spaces, overhanging roofs, indoor recreational spaces, and strong horizontal lines as well as a garage integral to the house. Ironically, the Robie family only lived there for 2 ½ years. Although the itinerary omits any Mrs. Robie, the design of this home so influenced American homes it merits inclusion.

See also the following key properties not included in the NPS travel itinerary (special thanks to Peg Strobel).

• Sears Building, the 100-story Sears Tower, once the world's tallest skyscraper, was the company headquarters for the major 1984-1985 EEOC sex discrimination suit against the world's largest retailer. Both sides hired historians of women to argue their cases. Sears won.

• Glessner House, home of Frances and John Glessner. Frances Glessner was an artisan and a key person in Chicago's Arts and Crafts Movement; they decorated their 1885 home using Arts and Crafts principles. The museum also interprets their servants' lives.

• The Haymarket Monument. Lucy Parsons fought to erect the 1893 Haymarket Monument in Waldheim Cemetery, Illinois, to the memories of the Haymarket Martyrs, including her husband Albert who was executed for his participation in the "Haymarket Affair." Nearby, "Dissenters Row" has the graves of labor organizers Emma Goldman and Elizabeth Gurley Flynn.

• Bahai Temple, Wilmette (north of Chicago). Corinne True played a major role in building the temple, spreading the Bahai faith in the U.S., and increasing women's participation.

• Frank Lloyd Wright Home and Studio, Oak Park. Marion Lucy Mahony Griffin, a renowned Prairie School architect, artist, and one of the first licensed female architects in the world, worked with Frank Lloyd Wright for fifteen years as a designer here.

• Jane Addams Hull-House. Founded in 1889 by Nobel Peace Laureate Jane Addams and Ellen Gates Starr, for decades Hull-House served as an essential locus of social reform and research while providing access to the arts and social services for its immigrant neighbors. The complex once occupied an entire city block with its many functions, including resident housing, educational classes, recreational activities, gender-based occupational training, and artistic programs.

• Ida B. Wells-Barnett, journalist, activist known for her indefatigable battles against lynching, lived in her Chicago Bronzeville home, now a National Historic Landmark, from 1919 to 1929. She was active on the national board of the National Association for the Advancement of Colored People (NAACP).

• Frances Willard home in Evanston, also the headquarters of the Women's Christian Temperance Union, a nationwide organization of women fighting for many women's issues, including alcohol abstinence and women's suffrage. Their motto was, "Do Everything."

• Wilmette, Illinois, named for a French fur trader and his part-Potawatomi wife, Archange Chevallier Ouilmette, who gained 1,280 acres from the U.S. government for their part in negotiating an 1829 treaty transferring many thousands of acres of tribal lands to the U.S.

- Illinois Prairie Path, founded by May Petrea Theilgaard Watts (1893-1975), a teacher, environmental educator, and author who also served as a naturalist (1942-1957) at the Morton Arboretum.
- Gerber/Hart Library, named in part after civil liberties lawyer Pearl Hart, was founded in 1981 as a depository for lesbian, gay, bisexual, and transgender individuals' and organizations' records. It now presents many programs and events and houses over 14,000 volumes, 800 periodical titles, and 100 archival collections.

Detroit, Michigan

- Pewabic Pottery was built in 1907 for ceramic artist Mary Chase Perry, who worked to raise American ceramic standards.
- Cranbrook Educational Community, a unique 300-acre campus begun in the 1930s, sought to be an artistic community to bring good design into everyday life, came from the partnership between Finnish architect Eliel Saarinen and *Detroit News* owners George and Helen Booth.
- Women's City Club building. Club members organized for the World War I home front effort, prohibition, and women's suffrage. They held classes and extensive recreation programs for over 8,000 Detroit women.
- Dunbar Hospital, opened in 1917, provided hospital care and nursing classes for growing numbers of African Americans moving to Detroit as part of the Great Migration from the South.
- Palmer Park Apartment Building Historic District has 40 multiple story units built between 1920 and 1940 for middle-class and upper-middle-class tenants.

Hardin, Iowa: Silos to Smokestacks

- Edgewood School of Domestic Arts, founded in 1886 by Eva Harrington Simplot, taught young women sewing, cooking, laundry, millinery, etc., all designed to "help people help themselves" in the Progressive era philosophy.
- Alden Public Library, a 1914 Carnegie-endowed library, sought to improve society with education and knowledge for the "masses."
- Union Cemetery Gardener's Cottage, a Craftsman building, was constructed in 1918 by the cemetery's owners, the Ladies' Social Gathering of Iowa Falls.

Indianapolis, Indiana

- Indianapolis travel itineraries include the following: Capital at the Crossroads of America, Ethnic Indy, Go Diagonal, Going in Circles, Neighborhoods in a City of Homes, Monumental Indianapolis, Feel the Need for Speed in Indy, and George Edward Kessler and the Park System.
- Cottage Home Historic District preserves a community of wood frame vernacular worker houses from the late 19th century, typical of this period in Indianapolis. First platted in the 1860s, these workers' cottages were built near the Bellefontaine Railroad repair shops.

Residents who also worked as policemen, firemen, house painters, and mechanics lived here with their families.

• When Sarah Breedlove (1867-1919) married, she took the name Madame C. J. Walker and developed the highly successful Walker System of hair and beauty products for African American women, creating job opportunities for them as hairdressers and sales agents. Walker became a millionaire and philanthropist and built herself a mansion, Villa Lewaro, in New York. Her daughter A'Lelia Walker built the Walker Building, the company's headquarters, in 1927.

• City Market served as the main public market for Indianapolis for over 120 years, where male and female vendors sold their wares before supermarkets became common.

• Crispus Attucks High School, opened by the Indianapolis School Board in 1927 as the first and only public high school for African American boys and girls in the city. The black community took pride in the school, where a black faculty taught black history. (Before, and after the 1970s, blacks attended high school with whites.)

• Lockefield Gardens Apartments completed in 1937 was one of the first Public Works Administration (PWA) projects in the nation. As blacks were particularly hard hit during the Great Depression, Indianapolis leaders requested a (PWA) grant to construct new apartment housing to eliminate deteriorated housing. Black families lived in them into the 1970s.

• Michigan Road Tollhouse provided housing for 25 years during the late 19th century for Samuel Howard and his family, who lived in the small company-built frame house while serving as toll collector for the Michigan Toll Road, and as storekeeper, postmaster, and notary public for travelers and nearby farmers.

Lexington, Kentucky: The Athens of the West

• Mary Todd Lincoln's childhood home, where she lived from age 14 (when not away at boarding school) to her departure to Springfield, Illinois, to live with her sister, and later marry Abraham Lincoln.

• Lexington Laundry Company and Embry's Department Store, two early 20th-century commercial services. The downtown commercial district changed women's lives by providing greater convenience and more consumer goods.

• Lexington Opera House, opened in 1887, where Mae West performed.

Lewis and Clark Expedition (1804-1806)

• Sacagawea, a 16-year-old Shoshone woman, with her baby son and husband Toussaint Charbonneau, joined the Corps of Discovery at the Mandan/Hidatsa village, now part of the Knife River Indian Villages National Historic Site, where the expedition set up its 1805 winter headquarters. She guided them, carrying her son along and showing that their expedition came peacefully.

• Corps leader William Clark tended men and women Nez Perce patients later in their journey.

Maritime History of Massachusetts

• Merrill's Wharf Historic District, in New Bedford. Landing place for Steamship Authority boats to the Massachusetts coastal islands of Nantucket and Martha's Vineyard for over a century, taking residents, vacationers, and tourists back and forth—including women!

Ohio and Erie Canal National Heritage Corridor

• "Society of Separatists of Zoar," a communal society in 1819 where men and women had equal political rights, paid off their land purchase by digging seven miles of the Canal. Later they owned four canal boats and by mid-century acquired more than $1 million in assets.

• May Company, Ohio's largest department store, had one million square feet inside.

• The Jones Home for Children, an independent orphanage and foster care home from 1886 to 1996, founded by Carlos and Mary Jones after their only son died.

Places Where Women Made History

75 sites in New York and Massachusetts

New York

• Emma Willard School/Troy Female Seminary, this country's first secondary school for females, came from Emma Willard's (1787-1870) pioneering efforts to expand educational opportunities for women. She opened the Middlebury Female Seminary in 1814 and the Troy Female Seminary (high school) in 1821, graduating more than 200 female teachers, including Margaret Slocum Sage (Russell Sage's wife and America's foremost woman philanthropist).

• Margaret Sanger Clinic. As a nurse on New York City's crowded Lower East Side, Margaret Sanger (1879-1966) saw the toll on women's health and the infant mortality from women not being able to control their fertility. She became an outspoken advocate for birth control and family planning, was arrested and tried for publishing articles on it. This clinic operated from 1930 to 1973, serving patients and teaching doctors contraceptive techniques when few medical schools did.

• Triangle Shirtwaist Factory Building, New York City, a clothing factory employing mostly women, known for its poor conditions and labor strife. Here, in 1911, 146 women died when it burned, many jumping to their deaths to escape from the fire. Public outrage and Frances Perkin's work led to greater safety codes.

• Henry Street Settlement and Neighborhood Playhouse, an early U.S. settlement, was founded in 1895 to treat the miserable urban conditions faced by poor New York City immigrants and workers. Its founder Lillian Wald, who saw first-hand the squalid conditions, organized a nursing service that led to public health nursing. Today it provides city residents numerous services and programs.

• Harriet Tubman Home for the Aged in Auburn opened in 1908 to house elderly women, the "last work" of Harriet Tubman (1820-1913), the famed African American Underground Railroad conductor credited with helping 300 slaves escape.

• Antoinette Blackwell (1825-1921) childhood home, a farmhouse where the first woman ordained in a U.S. church grew up. She attended Oberlin College and was ordained a Congregational minister in 1853, later becoming a Unitarian. Author, lecturer, feminist, she had seven children and a 65-year marriage.

• Cold Spring Harbor Laboratory Historic District, where Barbara McClintock worked. Her genetic research recognizing that genes can sometimes "jump" in reproduction won her a Nobel Prize.

• Barbizon Hotel, a 23-story New York City building, provided socially accepted (if carefully restricted) housing for women moving to New York for its new professional opportunities of the 1920s. With its Codes of Conduct and Dress enforced, it provided space for many social, intellectual, and athletic activities.

Massachusetts

• Emily Dickinson's (1830-1886) family home in Amherst, where she wrote her famous poems. She chose isolation, writing poetry from the 1850s barely known until after her 1886 death when her sister found hundreds of poems only later published.

• Cambridge Young Women's Christian Association (YWCA) building provided wage-earning women with low-cost housing, reading rooms, gymnasiums, and classes during the late 19th to early 20th centuries. Single women working in Cambridge, then a busy industrial center, had few places to live that would protect their "virtue" and "womanhood." Built in 1891, this YWCA had an employment office, vocational guidance, and classes in subjects from cooking to watercoloring, German, and the Bible.

• Julia Ward Howe (1819-1910) lived in this Boston home from 1863 to 1866 with Samuel Gridley Howe (1801-1876), her husband and fellow humanitarian and abolitionist during an extremely exciting period in their lives. She had recently composed the "Battle Hymn of the Republic," to the tune of "John Brown's Body," which made her quite famous. Later she fought for women's suffrage, peace, and pure milk for babies.

• Lancaster Industrial School for Girls, founded in 1854, was once a "most progressive correctional institution," a cottage system emphasizing a wholesome, family-like atmosphere where girls could rise above the "low life" slums that Victorians assumed caused delinquent children.

• Home of Mary Baker Eddy (1821-1910), founder of the worldwide religion Church of Christ, Scientist, in Lynn and author of *Science and Health with Key to the Scriptures;* this house was an early meeting place for the church she founded.

• Lois Lilley Howe (1864-1964) home, designed by the first woman architect elected a Fellow of the American Institute of Architects. She established one of the longest lasting and most prolific women's architectural firms with Eleanor Manning and Mary Almy focusing on urban housing.

• African American school principal Maria Baldwin (1856-1922) home. In 1882 the African-American community pushed for her hiring as a primary school teacher at Agassiz Grammar School in Cambridge, Massachusetts. Seven years later she was appointed its principal. In 1916, she became Master of the school with its new larger building. As Master, she supervised 12 white teachers with a 98% white student body. Only two women in the Cambridge school system held the position of Master; Baldwin was the only African-American Master in all New England. She was also a civic leader and lecturer.

• Major Joseph Griswold Home, where Mary Lyon (1797-1849), Mt. Holyoke College founder and pioneer in women's education, held classes teaching young women Latin, science, and history instead of the usual needlework and painting. She taught there for seven years until she opened a women's "seminary," soon Mt. Holyoke College in South Hadley, Massachusetts.

• Ellen Swallow Richards (1842-1911) house, Boston. This 19th-century advocate for public sanitation and good health is now recognized as the woman who created the fields of ecology and home economics, applying scientific principles to daily life and improving the sanitation and efficiency of homes. This house served as her laboratory and as an office for the Center for Right Living. Despite her eventual fame, Richard's hopes for a higher education were frustrated until, at the age of 25, she entered Vassar College and studied under Maria Mitchell. In 1873, MIT awarded Richards a B.S. degree as the first woman to graduate from a scientific school. But despite years of graduate study, she was never awarded the Ph.D. she earned.

• Eleanor Boit (1848-1932) house in Wakefield, Massachusetts. Boit was a businesswoman, the 1889 founder of the Harvard Knitting Mills, and director of a local bank. Once a textile factory worker herself, the textile company she founded provided employees with health care, vacation, sick leave, and profit sharing long before other companies. Her 850-employee firm produced 24,000 garments each day.

Pipestone, Minnesota

Except for Geyerman's, a woman's clothing store (1936-1964) in the Syndicate Block, and the third floor of the Masonic Temple where women's housedresses and aprons were manufactured from 1919 to 1920, women apparently did not live or work in Pipestone, a railroad and quarry town in southwestern Minnesota. No women are mentioned in its hospital (nurses?), Carnegie Library (librarians?), opera house (opera singers?). Pipestone Indian School, whose Superintendent's House remains of the once 60 building school with its 400 students–Dakota, Oneida, Potawatomi, Arickarree, Sac, and Fox–although one may assume there were female students because the school taught baking, cooking, and nursing. The "John Rowe House," noted as a common bungalow in unusual materials being sided with locally quarried Sioux quartzite, seems only occupied by Mr. Rowe. Certainly women lived there; clearly they are now invisible.

Puerto Rico and the U.S. Virgin Islands

Various families are mentioned in the 52 sites as well as plantations and missions, but the only specific woman mentioned by name is Charlotte Amalia, the Danish Queen whose misspelled name is St. Thomas Islands' town Charlotte Amalie. Moravians symbolically named their mission "New Herrnhut" in honor of their Mother Church in Germany; their missions built manses (homes) for the missionaries, but without any mention of female missionaries living in them. The Parroquia del Espíritu Santo y San Patricio's (Parish of the Holy Spirit and St. Patrick) massive walls sheltered its *people* from hurricanes and floods. Historical evidence shows female slaves lived on these plantations, with their astronomically high death rates. But not one of these entries identifies women there—whether indigenous, enslaved Africans, or immigrant Europeans, even though other evidence documents their presence.

Raleigh, North Carolina: A Capital City

• St. Mary's Episcopal school for girls, founded in 1842, provided education for Southern females when public education was unavailable.

• St. Paul AME Church, whose 25-year construction of an elegant new brick church stands as a tribute to its African American congregation who were paid very low wages as washerwomen, maids, nurses, and cooks.

• St. Agnes Hospital (1909) and Training School for Nurses established to provide medical care for and by African Americans during the Jim Crow era when hospitals were segregated by race.

• Grosvenor Gardens Apartments, built 1934-1939, provided a cross between houses and apartments for families facing a severe housing shortage; designed to provide outdoor play areas for children.

Richmond, Virginia

• First African Baptist Church originated when whites from First Baptist moved to a new church, leaving their old shared church to blacks in the congregation. The foremost black church in Richmond, with 1,400 marriages, 2,500 funerals and 5,800 baptisms during the Rev. James Holmes being pastor (1867-1900). Maggie Walker was baptized and married there.

• Broad Street Commercial Historic District, once core of Richmond's commercial district. After 1889 trolley lines ran down its middle, with shops and department stores along its length. Broad Street also included the Masonic Temple, the Richmond Dairy, the Empire Theatre, and the Central National Bank Building. From 1905-1911, the African American St. Luke Emporium was located here until white opposition closed it.

• Jackson Ward Historic District, a city-within-a-city during the Jim Crow period, was home to the African American Independent Order of St. Luke and its leader Maggie Lena Walker, whose home is part of the

National Park System and whose national headquarters, the St. Luke Hall, still stands. Many post-Civil War Baptist churches, including Sixth Mt. Zion, Ebenezer Baptist, and Sharon Baptist, lodges, insurance companies, banks, and schools, all served African Americans here as well as the Hippodrome theatre, the Eggleston/Miller hotel, and the A. D. Price Funeral Home. The St. Luke Building housed the banking, printing, insurance, and meeting functions of the 24-state "womanist" Independent Order of St. Luke.

• Ellen Glasgow House, a National Historic Landmark home of southern novelist Ellen Glasgow (1873-1945), who won the 1942 Pulitzer Prize for her final novel (of 19), *In This Our Life*.

• Virginia Union University, a historically black college founded in 1896 from several smaller African American colleges, provided higher education to men and women students. Coeducational, like most black colleges such as Hampton University and Tuskegee, VUU served its community when white schools refused blacks admission.

• Barton Heights Cemeteries has six African American burial grounds established by black churches and fraternal organizations, including the Daughters of Ruth and the Independent Order of St. Luke (with male and female members but strong female leadership).

Santa Clara County: California's Historic Silicon Valley

• José Maria Alviso Adobe, constructed 1837 with a major remodeling completed by 1853 by José Maria Alviso and his wife Juana Francisca who added a wood-frame second floor to the family's one-story adobe house.

• Winchester House, an enormous 160-room Victorian Mansion built by Sarah L. Winchester (1884-1922), wife of rifle manufacturer William Winchester. Influenced by a spiritualist, as a widow she continued to build and build—its construction only ending when she died; also called the Winchester Mystery House.

• Yung See San Fong house ("Young's Home in the Heart of the Hills"), built in 1917 by writer and playwright Ruth Comfort Mitchell Young and Sanborn Young, her environmentalist husband, who incorporated Chinese influences and ecological ones. Her campaigning is credited for his election to the California State Senate.

• Lou Henry Hoover and Herbert Hoover House, a large, rambling International style house, was designed by Lou Henry Hoover, geologist, relief worker, and former first lady.

Shaker Historic Trail

Connects many of the original communities associated with the United Society of Believers in Christ's Second Appearing, commonly known as the Shakers. The group was founded by "Mother" Ann Lee (1736-1784), its English-born leader who in 1780 sought to establish "heaven on earth" in America through practicing shared ownership, pacifism, celibacy, and gender equality—beliefs that challenged mainstream American culture. Their legacy is preserved in many of their original communities, such as Canterbury Shaker Village, Hancock Shaker Village, and Mount Lebanon. Only the Sabbathday Lake, Maine, community remains active.

Seattle

Like these other itineraries, women remain "missing" and often invisible—the Times Building had a an information line, where numerous telephone operators answered questions on any topic, the Queen Anne High School had students, and the Cobb Building housed both dental and medical facilities. In all these places, as well as the various residences, one can reasonably expect women and girls to have been there—but this itinerary focuses the story of Seattle on its wealthy business men and architects.

• The Arctic Building had a ladies' tearoom and provided an exclusive social community for those Seattleites who had returned from the Alaska Gold Rush with money in their pockets. The Flatiron Building later housed a brothel.

• At the turn of the 20th century, hills south of downtown Seattle had hundreds of multi-family rental houses. Only the Victorian Apartments built in 1891 remain as an unaltered example of a pre-20th-century wooden apartment building. *Historic Seattle* established a partnership that allowed the Victorian Apartments 83-year-old owner to remain in her long time home.

• The Harvard-Belmont District, an exclusive residential area, with 45 large houses, includes the Century Women's Club in the neighborhood.

• The Boeing Company, which built World War II's famous B-17 and B-29 bombers, outgrew the ground floor of its Red Barn as the company became a key Pacific Northwest industry. Today the Museum of Flight occupies the building. That museum shows two young girls and their puppy as Boeing 247 passengers in the 1933 first modern passenger airplane and also as Pacific Airlines stewardesses outside a pre-jet age propliner. The museum has a 1934 United Air Lines Flight Attendant uniform, when stewardesses were required to be registered nurses! Women also built bombers during World War II there.

• Columbia City boomed in the 1920s, when Seattle residents reached their vacation homes along nearby Lake Washington by streetcars. The town later became ethnically diverse, with Italians, Japanese, African Americans, Filipinos, Latinos, Vietnamese, and East African immigrants all living there. The Highlands neighborhood developed in 1914 and quickly became a popular for wealthy Seattle's summer homes.

• International District (Seattle Chinatown Historic District) combines American, Chinese, and Japanese design where immigrants established companies and neighborhoods. Differences in immigration laws towards the two Asian groups greatly affected their lives, especially their women's lives.

South and West Texas

• Ursuline Academy, built in 1851 for the Ursuline nuns who came from New Orleans to strengthen the Roman Catholic Church in Texas after it gained independence from Mexico. Today, the Academy, Dormitory, and Academy Chapel remain; the academy operated here until 1965.

Three Historic Nevada Cities: Carson City, Reno, and Virginia City

Carson City

• Stewart Indian School, 83 buildings (1890-1980), an off-reservation boarding school for students from many western tribes to force their assimilation and teach them trades. After 1934, student treatment changed and the school encouraged its students to retain their tribal cultures.

Reno

• Riverside Hotel, a popular, elegant, and well-known hotel conveniently located next to the Washoe County Courthouse. It featured six floors of rooms for couples getting "Reno divorces" (1920s-1960s) after Nevada passed a 1931 divorce law that only required a six-week residence.

• 20th Century Club, built in 1925 as Reno's first women's club, was open to all women "of good repute." Its members worked for many causes; in its rooms many community functions, from meetings to weddings, happened.

Virginia City

• By 1880, with one-third of the population under 18 years old, Virginia City became more a family-based community than a stereotypical mining boomtown. The Fourth Ward School built in 1876 housed 1,025 students, grades 1-12, until it closed in 1936.

Washington, D.C.

Mary Church Terrell (1863-1954), Memphis-born Oberlin College graduate was a teacher, organizer, author, founder and first president of the National Association of Colored Women, National Association for the Advancement of Colored People (NAACP) Executive Committee founder, and suffragist—always fighting to improve black women's lives. At age 86, she protested against segregation at Thompson's Restaurant in the nation's capital, suing it and winning blacks access to public eating places. She became more militant after the death of her husband, Robert Terrell.

• Cleveland Park, a streetcar suburb, had most of its single-family homes and some apartment buildings built between 1894 and 1930.

• DAR Constitution Hall built by the National Society, Daughters of the American Revolution (DAR), to house their annual Continental Congress and other activities. Founded by descendants of soldiers who fought for the Americans in the American Revolution, the hall also served as an unofficial Washington, D.C., cultural center for over forty years. When the DAR denied use of its Hall to African American singer

Marian Anderson, First Lady Eleanor Roosevelt intervened and made the Lincoln Memorial available for Anderson's 1939 Easter concert.

• Sewall-Belmont House, a block from the U.S. Capitol, has been the headquarters of the National Woman's Party (NWP) since 1929. Home of Alice Paul (1885-1977), suffragist, Equal Rights Amendment author (in 1923!), and strategist responsible for including women in the 1964 Civil Rights Act. A National Historic Landmark, museum, and library.

• Old Stone House, Georgetown built by Christopher Layman, was initially a one-room home for Rachel Layman and her husband before being sold to a wealthy widow, Cassandra Chew, who added a wing to the rear of the house in 1767 and a second floor. Chew lived in the upper floors and rented out the first floor. When she died in 1807, she willed the house to her daughter.

• The Lockkeeper's House, the only visible remnant of the C & O Canal Extension, was built for the canal's toll collector. Near the Washington Monument, a 19th-century photograph shows an elderly black couple sitting just outside it.

• Woodrow Wilson House, a mansion near Dupont Circle where the president, partially paralyzed from a stroke he suffered in 1919, spent his few remaining years in seclusion under the constant care of his wife Edith Bolling Galt Wilson and their servants.

• Mt. Zion Cemetery. In 1816, the black members of the Dumbarton Street M. E. Church formed the Mount Zion Methodist Church, taking over the cemetery in 1879. Created in 1842, the Female Union Band Society, a cooperative benevolent society of free black women whose members pledged to assist one another in sickness and in death, purchased the land for the burial ground that year. Mt. Zion Cemetery illustrates the significant contribution African Americans made to the development of Georgetown and the important role an early black women's benevolent society played in their lives.

• Dunbarton Park, where Mr. and Mrs. Robert Woods Bliss, owners of Dumbarton Oaks House, hired the renowned landscape architect Beatrix Jones Ferrand (1872-1959) to design and build the "masterful and delightful" 10-acre formal gardens around their house. She designed estate garden landscapes; at Dunbarton Oaks she created intimate spaces and sweeping vistas, using pergolas, terraces, specimen trees, and benches. A species of forsythia has been named after her.

• Dunbarton House, headquarters of the National Society of Colonial Dames of America, a patriotic women's organization founded in 1891 to collect and preserve historic objects and to educate citizens. The society purchased this early 19th-century federal style house to preserve it. First built during "the heady days when the country and capital were new" [NSCDA website], the house sheltered Dolley Madison after she fled the White House before the advancing British troops during the War of 1812. She didn't want to be captured by them.

• The Volta Laboratory and Bureau building, a National Historic Landmark, constructed in 1893 by Alexander Graham Bell for his work assisting deaf and hearing impaired people. Bell, who had patented the first telephone in 1876, came from a family of educators of the deaf; his wife Mabel Hubbard had been deaf since early childhood. Here Bell continued his efforts "for the increase and diffusion of knowledge relating to the Deaf."

• Octagon House, where Dolley Madison and her husband, President James Madison, lived after the British burned down the nearby White House during the War of 1812.

• Arlington House, known as home for Robert E. Lee and his family; their enslaved housekeeper Selina Gray protected it during the American Civil War. A Freedmen's Village was built on its grounds.

We Shall Overcome: Historic Places of the Civil Rights Movement

• Daisy Bates (1914-1999) House in Little Rock, Arkansas, an ordinary home of an extraordinary African-American woman who guided and supported the Little Rock Nine (6 girls, 3 boys) as they desegregated the Central High School in 1957 against fierce white opposition. President of the Arkansas NAACP and co-publisher with her husband of the *Arkansas State Press,* she mentored the students. Her home served as both command post and haven for them.

• Little Rock High School, now Central High School National Historic Site, symbolizes the often violent struggle over school desegregation. Only with federal intervention were the students admitted to the school where they faced ongoing hostility.

• Dexter Avenue Baptist Church, backbone of the 1955-1956 Montgomery, Alabama, bus boycott whose female teachers and working women played leading roles organizing that effort that lasted almost a year until the Supreme Court ruled Jim Crow bus segregation laws unconstitutional.

• Sixteenth Street Baptist Church in Montgomery, Alabama, where a Ku Klux Klan bomb killed four young African American girls one Sunday morning in 1963, setting off national outrage and strengthening the Civil Rights Movement. Addie Mae Collins, Denise McNair, Carole Robertson, and Cynthia Wesley died from the bombing that came without warning.

• Modjeska Monteith Simkins (1899-1992) house in Columbia, South Carolina, a civil rights advocate and public health reformer for African Americans. She worked as the Director of Negro Work for the South Carolina Anti-Tuberculosis Association improving black health until fired for her civil rights work with the NAACP. Her house also served as office, meeting place, and lodging for African American visitors shut out of the local hotels.

• *Brown v. Board of Education* National Historic Site, Topeka, Kansas, whose plaintiff-parents wanted their daughters and sons to be able to attend quality racially integrated schools, commemorates the several cases from states brought together before the U.S. Supreme Court resulting in that historic 1954 decision that found the "separate but equal" doctrine unfair and unconstitutional. See also www.nps.gov/brvb.

• Juanita J. Craft (1902-1985) house of the Texas civil rights organizer and public servant. In 1935, Craft joined the NAACP, starting 182 rural Texas NAACP chapters. She also integrated universities, the Texas state fair, theatres, restaurants, and lunch counters. Both Martin Luther King Jr. and John F. Kennedy consulted with her. In 1975, at age 73, she was elected to the Dallas City Council.

• Ida Bell Wells-Barnett (1862-1931) home in Chicago. She fought as a journalist, civil rights advocate, and suffragist and was especially known for her crusades against lynching (public ritualistic murder of African Americans by torture and hanging), segregation, and economic oppression. She and her husband bought the stone residence in 1919, living there until 1929.

• The Lincoln Memorial has been the site of civil rights demonstrations for over eight decades in spite of its segregated 1922 dedication. On Easter Sunday 1939, contralto Marian Anderson sang a concert to 75,000 people gathered there after the DAR had denied her use of its Constitution Hall. In 1963, when the Rev. Dr. Martin Luther King Jr. gave his "I Have a Dream" speech there, he hoped for a country free of racism for his sons and daughters.

• Elizabeth Harden Gilmore (1909-1986), a business leader, licensed funeral director, and civil rights activist, lived and worked in this house, also known as the Harden and Harden Funeral Home, from 1947 to her death. She formed a women's club, successfully integrated a local department store, helped black renters, and amended West Virginia civil rights laws. A friend said, "She was always there. Her commitment was ongoing and steadfast."

World War II in the San Francisco Bay Area

• Richmond Shipyard Number Three, where more than 747 vessels were built here in the four Richmond Kaiser Shipyards during World War II using a production line technique, bringing pre-made parts together, moving them into place with huge cranes, and having them welded together by "Rosies" (actually "Wendy the Welders" here in the shipyards). This process allowed unskilled laborers to do repetitive jobs requiring relatively little training, opening up jobs previously closed to women and minorities. In three years, people moved here from all over the U.S., increasing Richmond's population from 20,000 to over 100,000. Excited about earning money and helping the war effort, they also faced challenges as working parents (finding daycare and housing) as well as unequal pay, daily prejudice, and inequities that resulted in labor strikes and sit-downs. At its height, 24,500 women worked for the Kaiser plants, many of them working mothers.

• SS Red Oak Victory, built in Richmond Kaiser Shipyard #1, was launched on November 9, 1944. One of 414 Victories built during World War II, the SS Red Oak Victory served as an ammunition ship in the South Pacific. Many of the "Rosies" believed their jobs crucial in protecting the lives of their husbands, brothers, and sons; they took great care in their welds, as shown by welds still strong after 60 years. For more information, read the website essay "Tending the Home Front: The Many Roles of Bay Area Women during World War II."

• The Atchison Village Housing Project provided desperately needed housing for these home front workers who left their children in the Maritime Child Development Center, one of 35 such day care facilities there. The Kaiser Richmond Field Hospital served these employees through one of the first voluntary pre-paid medical plans until its 1995 closing.

For more information, see also:

• **American Association for State and Local History**: Professional support for museums and historic sites of all kinds and sizes; www.aaslh.org.

• **Library of Congress:** Manuscripts, maps, and photograph collections; excellent online resources; www.loc.gov.

• **National Archives and Records Administration:** Government documents; www.nara.gov.

• **National Council on Public History**: Organization serving those who research, preserve, interpret, and manage historic resources outside the traditional classroom and those who teach public history; www.ncph.org.

• **National Park Service:** Parks and programs; over 400 parks, plus 2,500 National Historic Landmarks and 50,000 properties listed on the National Register of Historic Places; technical guidance for historic preservation and cultural resources management; and publications. See www.nps.gov for parks and general information and www.cr.nps.gov for cultural resources, including history, architecture, landscape architecture, archaeology, ethnography, and museum curation.

• **National Trust for Historic Preservation:** Manages sites they own, publishes the magazine *Preservation,* advocates and provides professional support for historic preservation; www.nthp.org.

• **Organization of American Historians:** Public and academic historians; www.oah.org.

AND, OF COURSE . . .

• **The National Collaborative for Women's History Sites:** Support for and advocacy of women's history in many kinds of places. **http://ncwhs.oah.org.**

Happy traveling!

ACKNOWLEDGMENTS

We want to acknowledge and give special thanks to our contributors and partners. We could not have produced this guide without your help.

Dawn Adiletta, Mike Andrus, Joan Bacharach, Bill Barclay, Kevin Bartoy, Beth Grosvenor Boland, Maria Capozzi, Estelle Carol, Richard Carrillo, Ashley Carver, Nupur Chaudhuri, Charlie Clapper, Bonnie Clark, Dina Clark, Maria Cole, Paul Cole, Richard Colton, Maggie Cooney, Ellen Cronin, Eola Dance, Tricia Davies, Donna DeFalco, Dana Dierkes, Pam Elam, Jacsin Finger, Susan Finta, Susan Hill Gross, Louise Howard, Mary Jenkins, Mary Ann Johnson, Kevin Kissling, Carol Kohan, Carla Koop, Gretchen Kreuter, Julie Kutruff, Lucy Lawliss, Lisa Yun Lee, Martha Lee, Cynthia Little, Cynthia MacLeod, Franceska Macsali-Urbin, Molly Murphy MacGregor, Teri Mandic, Joan Meacham, Mary Melcher, George Minnucci, Bob Moore, Patricia Murphy, Kris Myers, Abigail Newkirk, Nancy Nelson, Leslie Obleschuk, Sarah Olson, Marea Ortiz, Lori Osborne, Robert Parker, Michael Regoli, Linda Riley, Vivien Rose, Dave Ruth, Pam Sanfilippo, Jan Sansone, Carol Schull, Susan Scott, Julie Siebel, Anthony Shahan, Steve Sitarski, Sherrie Smith-Ferri, Klydie Thomas, Catherine Turton, Sally Roesch Wagner, Judith Wellman, Patricia West, Stephanie Wolf, and Amber Young.

Heather Huyck, Peg Strobel, and Robert Cooney
Williamsburg, VA, Oak Park, IL, & Santa Cruz, CA

Join the NCWHS to help preserve and promote women's history sites

The **National Collaborative for Women's History Sites** (NCWHS) supports and advocates the preservation and interpretation of places, collections and organizations that bear witness to women's participation in American history. By making women's lives visible at historic sites, all women's experiences and potential can be fully valued—and our history can be truly understood. The NCWHS is a non-profit, 501 (c) (3) educational institution. Contributions are tax deductible. We welcome both organizational and individual members. Please visit our website, http://ncwhs.oah.org, for more information.

NATIONAL COLLABORATIVE FOR WOMEN'S HISTORY SITES
HTTP://NCWHS.OAH.ORG